The New University Library

The New University Library

Four Case Studies

MATTHEW CONNER

an imprint of the American Library Association
CHICAGO   2014

Matthew Conner has a PhD in American literature and an MLS in library science, both from the University of Illinois at Urbana-Champaign. He is currently an instruction/reference librarian at the Peter J. Shields Library at the University of California, Davis, and President-Elect of the Librarians Association of the University of California (LAUC). As chair of the LAUC Professional Governance Committee, he recently led a systemwide study of the future of the University of California libraries, which forms the basis of this book. He is also pursuing research on information visualization and the pedagogy of keyword searching, which he has reported on at numerous conferences and in an article in *Reference Services Review*.

© 2014 by the American Library Association

Printed in the United States of America

18 17 16 15 14   5 4 3 2 1

Extensive effort has gone into ensuring the reliability of the information in this book; however, the publisher makes no warranty, express or implied, with respect to the material contained herein.

ISBN: 978-0-8389-1193-8 (paper)

Library of Congress Cataloging-in-Publication Data

Conner, Matthew.

    The new university library : four case studies / Matthew Conner.

      pages   cm

  Includes bibliographical references and index.

  ISBN 978-0-8389-1193-8 (alk. paper)

  1. Academic libraries—United States. 2. Academic libraries—United States—Case studies. 3. University of California, Davis. Library—Case studies. 4. University of California, Merced. Library—Case studies. 5. University of Hawaii at Manoa. Library—Case studies. 6. University of Illinois at Urbana-Champaign. Library—Case studies. I. Title.

Z675.U5C7535 2014

027.70973—dc23

                                    2013044167

Cover design by Kimberly Thornton. Images © Shutterstock, Inc.

Text design by Maia Rigas in the Adobe Jenson Pro and Helvetica fonts.

♾ This paper meets the requirements of ANSI/NISO Z39.48-1992 (Permanence of Paper).

To my parents,

for their unwavering support through thick and thin.

Contents

⊞

Preface

■■

This book has a very personal beginning. At the end of 2009, while finishing out a term on the Committee on Professional Governance (CPG) of the Librarians Association of the University of California (LAUC), I received a call from the LAUC president asking if I would chair the committee through the next year for a new project. Along with the rest of the profession, the University of California (UC) sought to assess its position amidst the vast changes of a new millennium whose alarming instability had been brought into painful focus by the national economic recession of 2008. The economic effects were especially evident in California, which featured in the *Guardian* as possibly the first "failed state" of the Union (Harris 2009). Would I design a systemwide conversation on the future of the UC system libraries for the twenty-first century? I said yes.

As the first part of the charge, my committee was given a month to prepare a workshop for the annual assembly of the LAUC membership (encompassing the ten campuses of the UC system) at UC Berkeley to initiate the systemwide project. I began reading in earnest, and I found that there was a big difference between a passing familiarity with issues of the profession and a systematic study of them. As Samuel Johnson observed, "When a man knows he is to be hanged in a fortnight, it concentrates his mind wonderfully." To my consternation, I found that the library profession, which is almost synonymous with order, was, in its deliberations about itself, wildly unorganized. The future of the library is discussed from every possible angle: electronic versus print formats, books versus periodicals, the role of the Internet, the implications of copyright law, the habits and very brain function of a new generation of library users—the millennials—budgets, library education, any number of technologies, the library building facilities themselves, and far too many other topics to name. These issues are projected into the future in various degrees from the next few months to years and even decades. And the projections range from calls for rebirth and new frontiers to (more commonly) apocalypse and the end of librarianship and even of organized knowledge. To an extent, one might take all of this as a healthy ferment of research. But it certainly would not do for someone expected to talk coherently before a large number of people. And I suspect that everyone would gain from some basic shape to the conversation, or a set of priorities, or at least a few reference points.

Having completed one course in cataloging (about which more need not be said), I essayed a basic classification of topics to frame the professional literature. I ended up with nine categories: reference, scholarly communication, personnel, technology, collections, buildings, campus roles, library networks, and library culture. So much for a new classification system! Yet, this did not seem sufficient either. Projecting ahead (accurately as it turned out), I imagined a sea of upturned faces of librarians who had taken time from busy schedules to hear something of value. And with a sense of unease, it seemed to me that the professional literature, even neatly classified, was just not going to meet the expectations for it. If the literature has any common characteristics, they fall into two categories. One is an eager, prophetic mode that seems to grow more enthusiastic as it reaches farther into the future. Libraries will disappear, to be replaced by electronic delivery systems. Librarians will need complete retraining in business or technologies. The entire category of technical services will cease to exist! Such literature is highly speculative, and the very complexity of change that fuels these scenarios makes it unlikely that any of the predictions will be accurate. Anyway, they certainly wouldn't do any good to my audience. The second category is marked by a belief that there is no problem that cannot ultimately be swallowed up and dealt with through an appropriate networking and leveraging of organizations. (The term "networks" recurs frequently.) According to this logic, it seems that any problem can be administrated away simply by redrawing organizational charts and workflows. But while this sounds comforting in the abstract, I was left wondering just what this would look like to a line librarian. Not much, it appeared to me.

I concluded that not only was I not in a position to tell librarians about their profession but that there was probably no one who really could. Of course there are any number of qualified and knowledgeable people to give keynotes and presentations. But I thought here of a keynote speaker at the 12th National Conference of the Association of College and Research Libraries (ACRL) in Minneapolis in 2005. Dr. William J. Mitchell, Professor of Architecture and Media Arts and Sciences at MIT, claimed that his graduate students in seminar had taken to Googling his every statement

on the spot and coming up with rejoinders and counterclaims. The experience, he said, was "exhilarating" but "exhausting," and he realized that there
was no way that anyone could keep up with the whole world. Taking this
to heart, it seemed more appropriate that information should flow from
the line librarians to me and that there should be some mechanism for fa-
cilitating this transfer. It occurred to me to use the direct experience of the
librarians and the organization of the University of California, whose ten
campuses as envisioned in the Master Plan for Higher Education in California in 1960 would form a sort of utopia of higher education. The UC's
ten campuses are highly diverse and adapted to their environments, and as
such they provide a large slice of the experience of higher education.
Brought into conjunction, the ten campuses are a problem-solving machine for investigating different issues of the future and determining different directions. As reported through line librarians, their operation would
serve to check and assess theory about the profession and speculations
about its future. What emerged was a two-part program: reporting on theories and speculation about the future, and then testing these ideas against
the experience of working librarians. The annual meeting was a success,
and the ensuing yearlong study conducted through different venues was
fruitful enough that it seemed worth extending into a reflection on the
profession as a whole. Thus was the origin of this book.

One significant question of methodology is how to justify any set of
categories as a suitable frame for studying the profession. The categories
one chooses for analysis will inescapably determine the answers to a degree. How many categories should there be? Which are the right ones?
The debate could go on forever. The categories selected for the UC project
were conceived as a starting point to be winnowed and adapted if there
was a need. As it turned out, in the course of the year, the full slate survived and produced useful discussions. They also turned out to make a
close match with the ACRL Top Ten Trends for the Future of 2010.

1. Academic library collection growth is driven by patron
   demand and will include new resource types.
2. Budget challenges will continue and libraries will evolve
   as a result.
3. Changes in higher education will require that librarians
   possess diverse skill sets.
4. Demands for accountability and assessment will increase.
5. Digitization of unique library collections will increase
   and require a larger share of resources.

6. Explosive growth of mobile devices and applications will drive new services.
7. Increased collaboration will expand the role of the library within the institution and beyond.
8. Libraries will continue to lead efforts to develop scholarly communication and intellectual property services.
9. Technology will continue to change services and required skills.
10. The definition of the library will change as physical space is repurposed and virtual space expands. (ACRL Research Planning and Review Committee 2010)

And here are the categories for the UC project:

1. Reference
2. Scholarly communication
3. Personnel
4. Technology
5. Collections
6. Buildings
7. Campus roles
8. Library networks
9. Library culture

All but numbers 2 and 4 of the ACRL list fit exactly into the UC project list, and 2 and 4 are dealt with implicitly in the UC list. Even so, it is more important to have a framework than to decide exactly what it will be. Making the executive decision to have some categories enables reflection, which will turn up better categories or other modifications where necessary. For this book, categories 2 and 8, scholarly communication and library networks, were absorbed into the other seven.

In keeping with the rationale for the original project, this study tests theory against lived experience in the form of case studies. A second critical question, then, is, Which case studies to choose? The University of California as one single system should not be extended to the entire profession. Two libraries come to mind as natural choices. UC Merced (UCM) was the first major university built in the twenty-first century in the United States, and its library, in accordance with the rest of the campus, was built as the library of the future. It is an ongoing life-size experiment on the latest and most venturesome ideas in library design and service. The University of Illinois at Urbana-Champaign (generally known as Illinois, which I will use also to refer to its library) is a colossus of the library world whose collection size is among the very largest and whose associated library school, the Graduate School of Library and Information Science (GSLIS), has been consistently ranked as the best in the nation for many years. Illinois stands at the pinnacle of the profession and is the very paradigm of the traditional research library, with a vast collection and a decentralized departmental structure. Its efforts to grapple with change from the collection of print materials that has defined academic libraries to some new model will be instructive to any academic library. These two, juxtaposing newness and tradition and the small and the large, make up half of the case studies. What of the other two?

An academic library is a vast organization like a miniature city, and going into any depth at all requires great time and effort. Studies across institutions now are largely based on groupings of peers, defined generally from quantitative factors. I adapted the basic principle of familiarity, underlying this method, to use my knowledge of specific institutions, acquired through years of personal and professional exposure, as a starting criterion—though not the sole interest—for my remaining case studies. And where these selections may cross the boundaries of peer institutions, this is all to the good in reconsidering definitions that are frequently arbitrary anyway. By starting with the known as a stepping-stone to the unknown, such introspection repeated for institutions throughout the profession will give us a better sense of the work that we do. Furthermore, predicting the future is difficult to do. It seems more worthwhile to study the future in terms of how institutions are grappling with change now rather than investing in particular institutions as models of what will be.

Growing up in Honolulu, I spent many hours in the main library of the University of Hawai'i at Mānoa (UHM). And while I was far from an adept user of the library, I absorbed its campus environment and its unique island culture beyond what any project-based researcher could do. A midsized public university library, its location as a crossroads of the Pacific makes it of particular interest now. The always deep cultural sensitivity of the islands has fused with educational movements in multiculturalism to place the university library and its area collections at the forefront of cultural preservation. In a more literal sense, the library has engaged with its environment in the form of a catastrophic flood in 2004 that wiped out the basement floor and most of the government documents collection as well as other services. Such an invasive action and its aftermath had the effect of exposing the dynamic principles of the library in a way that is instructive for the profession.

The last four years of my career have been spent as an instruction librarian at the University of California, Davis (UCD). This has afforded me a vantage point for observing not just this library in transition but also the campus, the UC library system, and the entire state of California during a period of unusual turmoil. Paired with UCM, UCD offers an opportunity to meditate on the pros and cons of library networking within the largest and most cohesive public university system in the world. But perhaps the greatest value of UCD is one that it shares with UHM— neither one is exceptional (at first glance). Case studies of the unusual, while informative and thought-provoking, are not typical by definition. For the purposes of representation, it is more useful to have case studies of what seems normative. This material can be more readily generalized and, as I hope to show, is not normative at all upon closer inspection.

Taking off from the original project, this book examines seven professional trends, then tests them against the four case studies to match theory against practice. While the library profession favors hard data, preferably quantitative, in the current vogue for assessment, this study takes a slightly different tack. Appreciating librarians as the experts on their profession who combine training, professional knowledge, and the irreplaceable experience of running libraries, this study as much as possible relies on the voices of librarians themselves, talking about their work.

While this book essays a comprehensive view of the profession, a few words are in order about what it does not cover. The case studies are limited to academic libraries from medium to large universities that are publicly funded. One hopes that the findings will be relevant outside this scope to include other academic libraries and perhaps public libraries as well. But there are significant differences, too, between the libraries of large public universities and those at small liberal arts colleges or community colleges, and one should extrapolate to these and other situations with care. The book also does not treat cataloging and technical services work in much detail. In part this is because their detailed procedures are less important than their roles and organizational structures, which I do discuss. But it is also because there are others who are much better-equipped to discuss these topics than I am. Finally, space limitations require a regretful brevity in the treatment of initiatives of great richness and complexity. Instead, I invite readers to investigate further the programs discussed here, which are easily searchable online.

Acknowledgments

::

This project draws on my entire library career, so first I wish to thank David Wuolu and Ardath Larson, friends and colleagues, who got me started in librarianship at the University of Minnesota, Morris. For my case studies, I particularly wish to thank Randolph Siverson, David Michalski, Amy Kautzman, Xiaoli Li, and MacKenzie Smith at UC Davis; Donald Barclay and Jim Dooley at UC Merced; Paula Mochida, Martha Chantiny, Patricia Polanski, and Shanye Valeho-Novikoff at the University of Hawai'i at Mānoa; Paula Kaufman, Susan Searing, and JoAnn Jacoby at the University of Illinois at Urbana-Champaign, and far too many other librarians to name. If anyone had had the privilege to work with them as I did, they would feel very optimistic about the future of libraries. I also gratefully acknowledge research grants received from the Librarians Association of the University of California that allowed the completion of this book. Finally, I wish to thank Christopher Rhodes, J. Michael Jeffers, Rachel Chance, and Russell Harper, my editors at the American Library Association, for their invaluable encouragement and guidance.

Part One ∷ History

CHAPTER ONE

::

Overview

As custodians of the past, it behooves librarians to use the knowledge that they steward to understand the challenges they face. As the saying goes, in the past we may discern the present or even the future. Much current futurism assumes a historical vision that recurs frequently in the literature in the following form. From their very birth at the dawn of civilization, libraries served to collect and store knowledge, mostly for the purpose of the state or other institutions, not the public. Even the invention of the printing press in the early modern period had little effect on this pattern since the size of collections remained small. A new phase identified as modern librarianship began with the founding of the Boston Public Library in 1848. The emphasis remained on the storage and preservation of print documents. Yet collections expanded to become much larger, reaching into the millions of volumes in American libraries in the early twentieth century. And these materials were now thrown open to the public, as opposed merely to specialists. Academic libraries as one category of the profession followed the same developmental path, as we shall see. A third phase began at the end of the twentieth century and surrounds us now. This phase remains to be fully characterized. It is associated closely with the Information Revolution, which belongs on a level with the invention of writing and the printing press. Central to the new phase is the Internet, which makes vast amounts of information available to all. New technology has refashioned the learning and communications practices of a whole generation, reshaped the economy, and altered the very form of education and its structures of authority. The one thing that seems to be clear is that libraries will never be the same. In fact, for the first time in its history, the very existence of the library is being called into question.

Yet is this extreme scenario so certain? Some circumspect voices argue that predictions about the death or total reinvention of the library, like similar predictions of the end of books in the 1990s, are premature. More likely, these voices say, is a "hybrid model" in which libraries adopt some new technologies where useful while keeping the old (Pinfield et al. 1998). Yet another voice has argued that, in fact, libraries are based on a set of permanent principles and since their beginnings have never really changed at all (Thompson 1977, 11). Most of these principles sound surprisingly modern:

1. Libraries are created by society.
2. Libraries are conserved by society.
3. Libraries are for the storage and dissemination of knowledge.
4. Libraries are centers of power.
5. Libraries are for all.
6. Libraries must grow.
7. A national library should contain all national literature, with some representation of other national literatures.
8. Every book is of use.
9. A librarian must be a person of education.
10. A librarian is an educator.
11. A librarian's role can be an important one only if it is fully integrated into the prevailing social and political system.
12. A librarian needs training and/or apprenticeship.
13. It is a librarian's duty to increase the stock of his library.
14. A library must be arranged in some kind of order, and a list of its contents provided.
15. Since libraries are storehouses of knowledge, they should be arranged according to subject.
16. Practical convenience should dictate how subjects are to be grouped in a library.
17. A library must have a subject catalog. (Thompson 1977, 202–224)

Thompson also notes that the administrators have generally tended to be male while most librarians are female(!) (Thompson 1977, 103).

So we have the full spectrum of possibilities here. We are at a revolutionary new stage (or possibly the end of) libraries. Or we are in a new phase of growth that has some continuity with the past but moves in a different direction. Or nothing has really changed at all, and we are just seeing new manifestations of fundamental principles. How to choose among the possibilities? We can only look harder at history, to which we now turn.

Academic libraries in colonial America, according to one observer, provide a backwards look at the practices of the Middle Ages (Hamlin 1981, 25). Some limitations were imposed by the demands of settling a new continent. But libraries were also constrained by the educational system. Colleges essentially preserved the medieval subjects of the trivium (grammar, logic, rhetoric) and quadrivium (arithmetic, geometry, music, astronomy). The emphasis was on the maintenance of classical knowledge rather than innovation, and the mode of teaching was lecture-oriented and fundamentally hierarchical. Students listened and were expected to recite their lessons. There was little need for books at all. Accordingly, college libraries had small collections, mostly the result of private donations. The physical plant of the libraries consisted of a single room or sometimes even a set of cabinets. Rooms were unheated and virtually unusable during the winter for extended reading. In order to safeguard the books, no fire of any kind was allowed, so reading was possible only during the day. Libraries were typically open for a few hours a day or even on a weekly basis. In part, this was because the position of librarian was held in such low regard that he received little pay and, accordingly, was not disposed to keep long hours. Thus, added to the physical constraints, a culture operated whereby books were hedged about with barriers and made as inaccessible as the remote past that the students were supposed to imbibe (Rothstein 1976, 79). A case in point was the severe restrictions that surrounded the use of books themselves. Hamlin writes, "Pity the poor wretch who might be charged with injury to a volume while in his care; the regulations covering that problem go on interminably." It was the custom of students at Dartmouth College to express their resentment of overdue fines by throwing books downstairs (Hamlin 1981, 31, 36).

Nevertheless, the culture of academic libraries extended to a second, quite different system running in parallel with the official ones. University students reacted against their dull curriculums by compiling libraries of their own (Hamlin 1981, 38). This movement was assisted by the propensity of nineteenth-century Americans to form associations. Alexis de Tocqueville writes:

> Americans of all ages, all stations in life, and all types of disposition are forever forming associations. There are not only commercial and industrial associations in which all take part, but others of a thousand different types—religious, moral, serious, futile, very general and very limited, immensely large and very minute. . . . In every case, at the head of any new undertaking, where in France you would find the government or in England some territorial magnate, in the United States you are sure to find an association. (Tocqueville 1840, 513)

This trend was at work at colleges, where students formed literary and debating societies which charged members a fee to build up their own libraries. In contrast to the classical and historical works of university libraries, those of student societies emphasized novels, the natural sciences, and current topics. Many of these libraries outstripped those of the colleges. So a student-centered library culture thrived on its own, standing in the place of sports and other extracurricular activities which would arise later.

The year 1876 has been defined as the *annus mirabilis* of librarianship in America. The American Library Association (ALA) was founded that year, along with its companion publication, the *Library Journal*, as was a major source for specialized library equipment, the Library Bureau, founded by Melvil Dewey (fig. 1). The classification systems of Dewey and Charles Ammi Cutter were also both published that year. Dewey, indeed, was a colossus of the period; his innovations in every aspect of librarianship will be covered in more detail.

The accomplishments of 1876 meet most of the qualifications for a profession: an official organization, a body of standards and knowledge, and an official journal (Budd 2005, 62; Edgar 1976, 304; Hamlin 1981, 46; Rothstein 1976, 79; Carroll 1970, 9). This year of creativity for the library profession was also the start of modern academic librarianship, with the founding of Johns Hopkins University and its new vision of a library. But 1876 was as much the culmination of gathering trends as it was the fulcrum of innovation.

Many observers have noted the attraction of American universities to the German model (Rothstein 1976, 80). In contrast to the British model focused on teaching, the German model emphasized research by scholars, and this shift had profound ramifications. Research, most fundamentally, requires source materials in the form of books. The examination of books and the research they produced led to the seminar format,

Fig. 1. Melvil Dewey.

which displaced the lecture. For convenience, seminars needed their material readily at hand, and so private libraries were built that became the basis of departmental libraries. University libraries needed rapid expansion. They required larger collections, additional space to house the collections, more hours to access the materials, and a professionally trained staff to manage the larger, more valuable collections and guide users through them. The founding of Johns Hopkins University in 1876 is a convenient marker for the adoption of the German model in America, which took place over a period of time. The university's first president, Daniel Coit Gilman, was given a large endowment by eponymous benefactor Johns Hopkins to build a library suitable for the university. And such was the success of both the library and the university that they became models for other universities to follow (Budd 2005, 23; Hamlin 1981, 3; Rothstein 1976, 81).

Yet the foreign influence was not the only one. As part of the vast influence of the Civil War on American society, some have included changes to higher education (Hamlin 1981, 40, 47). Veterans as well as an entire society tempered by the war became less willing to follow tradition blindly. Students demanded more relevant subjects. Curricula and whole institutions were redesigned along the lines of efficiency based on the hard lessons of the war. And just as many of the volunteer associations of prewar society were absorbed into larger corporate structures, the libraries of student debating societies were typically absorbed into the collections of the university libraries.

Another American influence was Melvil Dewey. His lifetime of vast achievement and obsessive labor has been traced to his origins in a "burned-over" district of New York. The "burned-over" descriptor applies to successive waves of religious revivals that swept the region. While the various movements had different aims, they shared a general theme of reform and a religious fervor. The teenaged Dewey found himself musing in his journal about the "world work" that he would choose. Upon reaching adulthood, Dewey had determined that his goal was the reform of education in the broadest sense, and the rest is history; his defining contributions to librarianship were only part of his achievements. Dewey began work on his decimal classification system in his teens and revised it over the course of years as he applied it to various libraries. He was instrumental in founding the ALA, and he became one of its presiding members. He also founded the Library Bureau and helped to found the *Library Journal*. He moved on to become the head librarian at Columbia University. There, he dramatically expanded the size of the library collection, instituted the first reference service in an academic library, created an interlibrary loan (ILL) service, and inspired a new level of professionalization in libraries. Working with a system of five different colored fountain pens, he processed 550 pieces of mail a day. Moving on to become state librarian of New York, he created inspection systems that drove reform throughout the public school system. Dewey's relentless zeal, rooted in his religious upbringing and a certain Puritan streak, thrived in the expansion of the post–Civil War period and drove a professionalization of libraries that the original German model could hardly equal.

After 1876, the course of librarianship followed the broad outlines of the development of the nation. Academic librarianship had some differences from its counterpart in the public libraries but followed a similar trajectory. The post–Civil War era which saw the westward expansion of the country, and rapid industrialization saw the founding of new libraries, the construction of larger buildings, and the growth of collections. The original Morrill Act, which created land grant universities, became law in 1862 (Budd 2005, 22; Hamlin 1981, 46). Though suppressed in the short term by the Civil War, public state universities were becoming a powerful force in higher education. Libraries shrugged off centuries of lassitude and began building collections as fast as they could. Large collections drove not only technical developments, including innovations such as the card catalog and the metal multi-tier bookshelf, but also the formalization of cataloging rules. Librarians themselves became specialized, branching into technical and public services.

The period between the World Wars, even after factoring in the Great Depression, had little effect on libraries. Some budgets decreased, building projects were postponed, and some positions were closed. Yet libraries as a whole were buffered from the worst of economic hardship. Public libraries, in fact, enjoyed increased activity, as people retreated there for shelter, amusement, or information about jobs (Gambee and Gambee 1976, 175; Rogers 1976, 228).

The Second World War inaugurated a new phase of development. After the war's victorious conclusion, the revitalized American economy turned its energies to enjoying the fruits of peace. Funding for education increased, and the technologies created by war were applied at home. The Cold War, especially the launch of Sputnik, further energized the nation (Budd 2005, 28). More funding for libraries appeared, enhanced in the 1960s by Lyndon Johnson's Great Society programs. In the 1970s, however, funding began a long retreat that has continued to the present day and become markedly more pronounced with the economic crash of 2008 (Budd 2005, 4, 119). Meanwhile, technology continued to advance as a more and more capable servant of libraries. Library automation developed, and the personal computer appeared, enabling users to take advantage of electronic access. But with the rise of the Internet in the 1990s, technology broke its chains like Frankenstein's monster to become a serious competitor to libraries in ways that are still unfolding. This vast exfoliation of library development can be understood more fully in terms of our seven trends.

CHAPTER TWO

∷

Reference

Thompson makes the argument that education, if not reference specifically, has been one of the central goals of librarianship from its ancient beginnings. Scholars visiting the ancient library at Alexandria had largely unrestricted access to its vast collection, which implies at least some rudimentary service to guide users through it. Even prior to that, access was provided to Mesopotamian libraries whose texts of clay tablets were stacked and placed in pots according to an arrangement that is not understood; presumably some assistance was available there as well (Thompson 1977, 9). Nevertheless, reference in the modern era made a perceptible break with its past, and can even be traced to a single individual. Samuel Swett Green, librarian of Worcester, Massachusetts, has been called the father of reference. One of the founding members of ALA, he wrote in the first issue of *Library Journal* his famous statement reflecting the outward-looking service ethic of American public libraries. "You should not allow a patron to leave without having his question answered any more than a businessman would allow a customer to leave his store without purchasing something" (Rettig 2002, 18). Rather than guarding a collection, or even making it available, librarians were enjoined to seek out patrons and lead them to knowledge.

As one observer has noted, universities, with their long, "deadening" traditions, were insulated from the trends of public libraries (Gambee and Gambee 1976, 173). Nevertheless, reference in academic libraries had its own champion in Melvil Dewey. Part of his comprehensive plan for the modernization of the Columbia University library consisted of what has been recognized as the first academic library reference service (Hamlin 1981, 51). This involved supplying the best of what became standard tools—"bibliographies, cyclopaedias, dictionaries, and other works of reference" (Hamlin 1981, 143). To introduce users to these resources, he advised his librarians to cultivate a "condensed cordiality." This phrase digests debates that have continued to the present day over how aggressive librarians should be in offering service. Dewey seemed to be suggesting a balance between friendly approachability and efficiency. The whole method strikes one as a tool of business, typical of the man himself.

Dewey's reference model, however, had a subtler aim. Rooted in his life's work of reform and consistent with contemporary public librarians, Dewey sought to mold the very reading habits of his patrons to further their education (Wiegand 1996, 44, 89). This purpose became clearer when Dewey moved to his next position as state librarian of New York, where he sought to impose standards upon the entire educational system. At Columbia, he first built up the collection beyond previous levels, then facilitated its use by patrons. The same mission in the hands of contemporary public librarians bordered on the manipulative (Garrison 1979, 67, 91). In some cases, collections were arranged with what was considered "trash" such as romance novels placed in a way to entice readers along the shelves to what was considered valuable, ultimately philosophy and mathematics. But whatever the purpose, it is undoubtedly true that Dewey and his colleagues in public libraries made more books available to patrons than existed before.

Even Dewey's pioneering efforts in reference were subdivided in a way that is instructive to history. Because of his vast commitments, Dewey left much of the operation of his library school at Columbia to one of his subordinates, Mary Salome Cutler, who developed her own ideas about the role of librarians and the training that they needed. Cutler took exception to the mercantile idea of reference expressed by its "father" Samuel Green and adopted by Dewey: "It is sometimes said that the spirit of the library should be that of a merchant and his well-trained clerks, anxious to please their customers." Instead Cutler believed, "It should be rather the fine spirit of a hostess with the daughters of the house about her greeting guests." This "stereotypical orientation toward family and domestic tranquility exercised a warm and direct influence on librarianship" that was based on a "knowledge of books [the librarians] had read and of the community they wished to serve" (Wiegand 207). Accordingly, Cutler instituted a course of reading designed to enlarge the minds of the students and educate them beyond library procedures. Dewey canceled her course, but her values persisted and continue to inform reference service (Carroll 1970, 12).

Dewey's methodical procedures for reference (and tireless advocacy) spread throughout the profession. Yet the development of reference was driven too by the expansion of libraries and their growing collections. To make collections more available to its patrons, reference service subdivided in accordance with what the field of organizational development calls "differentiation" (French and Bell 1999, 91). As subject-specific seminar libraries were absorbed into the general collection, the libraries retained specialists who were expert in their specific collections. These departmental librarians were arranged into divisional groupings among the arts and humanities, sciences, and social sciences (Hamlin 1981, 140; Rothstein 1976, 89). As with the rest of librarianship, specialization emerged to keep pace with the growth and increasing complexity of libraries. This trend continued into the post–World War II era and even accelerated with the vast funds that poured into libraries as a corollary to the expenditures on education spurred by the Cold War and by Johnson's Great Society programs. At its height, reference service evolved the triage system. Its infrastructure had expanded the single reference desk that had first appeared into multiple desks in different parts of the library surrounded by specialized collections and staffed by experts (Burke 2008, 271). This mimicked hospital practice, which allowed patients to be routed efficiently to receive the care they need. In the library context, patrons are greeted near the entrance by an information desk. Staff answer simple repetitive questions such as where the restrooms and photocopy machines are located, where call numbers are located, and where to check out books. More complex reference questions are routed to the appropriate subject specialist desk. If the Great Society sought to extend opportunity to all parts of society, the triage reference model was its complement, providing maximum responsiveness and immediate service to patrons. But with the withdrawal of funding, reference service retreated.

Staff positions were frozen or eliminated and service points were closed. The larger difficulty, however, was external. For the last twenty years, reference usage statistics appear to show a steady decline on the order of a 2 percent annual decrease. This conclusion is surrounded by a fog within statistics itself. Given the variations across studies in time intervals, metrics used, types of libraries studied, and other variables, definitive numbers on the decline of reference become elusive. Nevertheless, there seems to be a consensus that a decline has been in effect for the last two decades at least (Applegate 2008, 176–178; Atlas, Wallace, and Fleet 2005, 314). This conclusion, however, unleashes more considerations that could change the meaning of the data. One is that the questions may have changed qualitatively from before. Rather than ready reference questions, which can now be answered from the Internet, patrons tend to ask more difficult research questions (O'Gorman and Trott 2009, 334). So the quality of questions may have gone up while the number has gone down. Or reference requests may be limited by reduced staffs, and individual staff may be busier than before (Applegate 2008, 184). Yet another point of view holds that a reduction in traditional reference shows the success of instruction programs that have sought to guide patrons in bulk. Patrons do not ask questions of reference librarians because they have already been answered through instruction (Zabel 2007, 109). But these theories remain speculative.

What seems certain, however, is that new information technologies have contributed to the decline of reference (Cardina and Wicks 2004, 133). When they search databases and retrieve content in full-text, patrons are eliminating two sources of questions—research and retrieval—for reference librarians. Even reference tools can be accessed online. *Britannica* and the *OED* (*Oxford English Dictionary*) are online, and *Wikipedia*, which has successfully challenged *Britannica* (in the results of a comparative study by the journal *Nature*), continues to grow in popularity (Giles 2005). Reference has been disintermediated!

Some wonder whether reference service even has a place in the future of libraries, although this service that emerged with the profession will not be given up easily. There has been a flurry of ideas for change, which (in a futuristic mode) can be classified into the categories of space and time. The category of space includes efforts to physically move the reference service out to patrons. Ideas here range from small, conservative modifications of existing practice to more radical ones (Gambee and Gambee 1976, 170; O'Gorman and Trott 2009, 327; Rudin 2008, 55). One idea calls for librarians not to sit at the reference desk, waiting for questions, but to move about, looking for opportunities to be helpful. "Some chose to interpret roving as simple, silent circling, wearing down a path in the carpet while waiting for students to signal their need, the passive roving approach. Others were more pro-active, using the broadcast method, announcing their availability huckster-style to individual students or to a cluster and waiting for takers" (Rudin 2008, 61). Similar versions eliminate a desk and call for librarians to walk through the library with laptops, ready to answer questions on the spot. More radical proposals call for moving reference service outside of the building. This can take the form of satellite desks in high-traffic areas such as student unions, dormitories, or departments. "Will librarians encamp themselves at the residence hall like colonial missionaries, trying to impose unwanted foreign values on the native population?" (Rudin 2008, 65). Some even call for "embedding," which, extending the liaison concept, moves an entire librarian position into an academic unit (Posner n.d., 3). The librarians become residents in the new location with their salary paid by the department or organization. These various proposals are being tried, and they have been scrutinized along every possible axis of inquiry. Roving librarians can be helpful or intrusive. Wandering, laptop-equipped librarians can be responsive but are cut off from any reference collection. Satellite reference points can reach out to new students but have also been ignored or inundated with trivial questions or queries unrelated to library resources. Embedded librarians are ignored as often as not, and in the current budget climate, it is unlikely that a department would fund a new library position. No one method has emerged as generally successful (O'Gorman and Trott 2009, 329).

The other category, time, includes proposals for asynchronous communication to provide service outside of working hours. The solution can be as low-tech as signage and handouts that address directional and other basic questions. Yet most of this class of proposals rely on technology. E-mail reference has been around for many years. But while it has been a useful supplement, it has not added significantly to reference statistics. Online tutorials and electronic kiosks are more recent but limited to the most basic questions. The most significant idea in this area is chat reference. In essence, this technology consists of a simple online chat whereby the librarian and patron share a real-time transcript. Some systems supplement the chat with preexisting scripts, knowledge bases of pre-answered questions, and methods for pushing web pages at patrons.

The chat service as a whole is driven by the mathematics of consortia. While a variety of chat widgets can be downloaded to individual workstations to make it functional, more expensive infrastructure makes other capabilities available such as those mentioned above and provides a means to send follow-up questions to various libraries and individual reference staff. Consortia are better able to pay for such technology than individual libraries, and most chat services operate through such networks. These chat services introduce both burdens and benefits, which, it is hoped, sum up to a net gain for participating libraries. On one hand, chat service extends reference hours. Some services, which are nationwide, can draw on staff to work outside of normal work hours, even 24/7, which would overtax the staffing of any single library. On the other hand, this blanket coverage comes at the price of service quality (Lapidus and Bond

2009, 138). Remote librarians may lack familiarity with other libraries and their procedures (King et al. 2006, 6). Frequently, firewalls block access to the resources of another library. Also, time and labor from a library's staff are siphoned off to assist a remote population. Meanwhile, the growing popularity of chat reference is the best indication of its effectiveness. However, usage statistics are still being compiled, and other modes of assessment have not yet emerged (Blank 2003, 222; Cardina and Wicks 2004, 140; Connaway and Radford 2011, 3; Cummings, Cummings, and Frederiksen 2007, 81).

A third idea for adapting reference services for the future goes beyond the categories of space and time to invoke a more philosophical concept that can be distilled into the image of the cyborg—combination organism and machine—which has been appropriated for cultural studies by Donna Haraway (Haraway 1991; Paula Kaufman makes a similar move in tracing the interrelations of carbon and silicon in the broadest sense [Kaufman 2007, 8]). Whereas cyborgs feature in movies and science fiction as futuristic and sometimes sinister creatures, Haraway argues that we are all cyborgs in our dependence on the technology that surrounds us—from word processors to online shopping, library catalogs, e-mail, social networks, and electronic access in general. Rudin employs this concept when she summarizes the goal of new reference as an effort to balance the imperatives of "high tech and high touch" (O'Gorman and Trott 2009, 329). The movement of physical reference service outward to additional spaces retains "high touch," but in some cases little is accomplished. Chat technology enables another form of coverage through "high tech," but service can suffer there as well. Even when the chat system is working correctly, it's hard to see it ever reproducing the full reference interview (Chowdhury 2001, 264; White 2001, 183). In the slogan of "high tech and high touch," we see reproduced the original debate between Melvil Dewey and his subordinate Mary Salome Cutler (Rettig 2002, 17). Dewey favored practically trained librarians who excelled at efficiently processing reference questions, while Cutler argued for deeper education of librarians and the treatment of patrons with warmth and understanding. The goal now is to retain a sense of humanity within our technology and continue the dialogue between Dewey and Cutler to provide the best reference service (Levrault 2006, 28).

CHAPTER THREE

Personnel

The permanent principles of librarianship invoked in chapter 1 contain one item especially relevant to the category of library personnel: librarians have always been educated. Equally relevant is the idea that libraries have generally been led by men with female subordinates (Thompson 1977, 102, 103). However, in America prior to 1876, librarians as a class had fallen into a condition of marginality where they were poorly paid and untrained (Budd 2005, 21). In some cases, their duties were entirely absorbed into other positions and carried out by a faculty or administrative staff members. The president of Yale's advice to his young librarian in the early nineteenth century captures a portrait of the profession.

> In regard to your leaving your place my thoughts have shaped themselves thus: the place does not possess that importance which a man of active mind would naturally seek; and the college cannot, now or hereafter, while its circumstances remain as they are, give it greater prominence. With the facilities you possess . . . you can in all probability secure for yourself . . . a more lucrative, a more prominent and a more varied, as well as stirring employment. I feel sure that you will not long content yourself . . . in your present vocation, and therefore I regard it better, if you must leave, to leave now, better I mean for yourself . . . (Hamlin 1981, 26)

The librarian in question was the young Daniel Coit Gilman, who, as the first president of Johns Hopkins, would one day lead a transformation of higher education based on an expanded role for the library. One wonders if his early experience at Yale fueled his drive for reform.

Another portrait of an individual that serves as representative of the profession, this time at the very cusp of change for academic libraries, concerns one B. R. Betts, librarian at Columbia University prior to Melvil Dewey. Betts guarded his collection with such zeal that he frequently returned money from the annual appropriations for books back to the university budget (Wiegand 1996, 78). He is reported by those who interacted with him as indifferent to the giving of information and positively irritated at being asked to retrieve a book. The university president, hoping for Columbia to participate in the changes taking place in higher education, grew impatient at his inaction and hired Dewey as replacement. The president's annoyance at Betts was seconded by another faculty member: "[O]ur mucilagenous librarian . . . the meekest and softest and least masculine of male mankind. Were a sea anemone or a jellyfish endowed with the faculty of speech, it would talk as he does" (Hamlin 1981, 173). While this estimate has none of the kindliness shown toward Gilman by the president of Yale, it duplicates a low estimate of the librarian's position. But Betts showed some fire at the end. When told that a more ambitious plan for developing the library would be forwarded to the Board of Regents instead of his own, Betts wrote that respect for himself and his position required his resignation. Thus passed an epoch of librarianship.

One of the defining features of a profession is an accepted means of training, educating, and certifying personnel, and to this extent, Dewey's creation of the first library school is another marker of the beginning of the library profession. The School of Library Economy that Dewey founded at Columbia lay outside the Regents' plans for the library, and he encountered resistance. Denied the space requested for the school, Dewey installed himself in an unoccupied room in a building near the library. Such maneuvering was the first of the willful, determined tactics that resulted in his eventual ouster from Columbia. In another act of defiance, Dewey opened his school to women, in violation of the university's ban on women students. His first class consisted of seventeen women and three men (Thompson 1977, 135).

While Dewey's dedication to reform is unquestioned, his admission of women, upon closer inspection, reveals the practical reasoning that was never far away from his missionary zeal. He needed students for his new school but had little incentive to offer in terms of support or prospects for employment. However, for women, excluded from the professions, Dewey's modest project provided an opportunity (Jackson 1974, 365). Dewey's choice of women students may also have been related to the controversies that surrounded him in later years for inappropriate familiarity with female employees, although no supporting evidence has been found. Rumors aside, both Dewey and his new female library students got what they wanted.

The women students played a significant role in the new reference service that Dewey opened at Columbia. The "Wellesley Half Dozen," six attractive and capable young graduates of Wellesley College, served as reference staff. Seeing women at all, much less ones of comparable age providing help in learning, was no doubt a heady experience for the young college students, and no doubt the women staff helped to popularize the service.

Yet again, a closer look at the library school reveals nuances in its contribution to the profession and to the status of women within it. Dewey set high professional standards. He insisted that the library students be not only punctual and diligent but also thoroughly grounded in the principles of cataloging, circulation, reference, and the many other details of operating a library. But while all of this aimed to bring knowledge to library users, he maintained the firm belief that the primary purpose of librarians lay in physically bringing books to the patron. Choosing this material and developing the collection he considered the duty of faculty and subject experts (no doubt through the specialization that was part of his modern vision). Therefore, some have argued, in the very process of establishing librarianship as a profession, Dewey forced it into a subservient role (Wiegand 1996, 372–373). These issues arose in Dewey's conflict with Mary Salome Cutler, who argued for deeper subject-based training for reference librarians. When their differences came to a head, Dewey made a show of surveying current and former library students about retaining Cutler's course. The students knew Cutler much better and wrote in support of her. After thanking respondents for their opinions, Dewey ignored them and abolished Cutler's course. Whatever Dewey's views toward the emancipation of women, they did not extend to a democratic procedure here any more than he considered subject instruction the responsibility of librarians.

While Dewey gained the loyalty of his mostly female library graduates, one could argue that they remained firmly within the boundaries of his professional view, which subordinated librarians to an inferior role within the university. This sense of status may be glimpsed in a poem published in the 1912 issue of the *Library Journal*.

> The A-L-Adies sailed one day,
> To voyage up the Saguenay,
> Gay and grim, stout and slim,
> Twenty-five hers to every him. (Garrison 1979, 146)

For those convinced of an image problem for librarians, this sample from the profession's flagship journal would seem to provide evidence. Women, whose presence was radical in Dewey's time, had become overwhelmingly dominant in the profession by 1912, but the status of librarianship had made them a target for jokes. (For more on gender in the history of librarianship, see Hildenbrand 1996.) It may be worth noting here the theory of "internalized oppression," which holds that one of the most powerful effects of oppression on a particular group is a reduction in that group's image of itself.

But in subsequent years, the status of the profession followed the growth of libraries on a steady upward track. Collections became larger, and staff expanded and differentiated itself to manage the collection and make it available to patrons. The next turning point can be found in the 1960s, the era that saw some of the greatest support for libraries, but also social turmoil. Just as the counterculture agitated and sought recognition for itself, so did librarians. Some have argued that the very prosperity of libraries played a role. As they came to control larger collections and to incorporate automation technology, librarians experienced both an increased sense of importance and a perceived loss of control to an abstract bureaucracy. In response, they began to demonstrate for recognition, often in opposition to the library director, who became identified with university administration. A movement to gain full faculty status, which had begun to emerge years earlier, developed into a vigorous campaign (Edgar 1976, 305; Hamlin 1981, 120; Rothstein 1976, 102). Librarians wished to have equal status with the professoriate with whom they worked. At the same time, the staff fractured from below. Nondegreed library staff who processed books now did the work that had been the province of librarians trained by Dewey but without similar recognition (Keys 1999, 172). The support staff sought to protect their rights with unions and were shortly followed in this example by the degreed librarians (Kaser and Jackson 1976, 130, 142).

Stresses on the staff structure grew with the long withdrawal of funding in the 1970s. Library automation required new skills with the arrival of the Internet and related communications technology by the early 1990s. Librarians found themselves in a changed world seemingly overnight. And just as librarians found themselves facing this global redefinition of their role, the accumulated reduction of positions over decades was aging the profession to an alarming degree. Half of all librarians today are due to retire in ten years. Not only did libraries not have positions; there were no librarians to fill them (Stoffle et al. 2003, 357, 373). The situation was so dire that the U.S. government proposed a $10 million initiative, administered by the Institute of Museum and Library Services, to recruit and educate librarians (Gorman 2003, 109).

At this point, whither the composition of library personnel? One popular way to track changes to library positions is to analyze advertisements for library jobs (Lynch and Smith 2001, 407). Current ads call for superlatives in a wide range of areas not commonly associated with librarianship. In addition to core skills, librarians must be good oral and written communicators, master sophisticated and ever-changing new technologies, and possess teaching skills, marketing skills, and business and managerial skills (Atlas, Wallace, and Fleet 2005, 315; Cardina and Wicks 2004, 134). Yet Brian Schottlaender, University Librarian at the University of California, San Diego, has put this in perspective by pointing out that, like many other dramatic-seeming changes to the field, the current demands have a long history (Schottlaender 2009). Namely, the call for librarians to be all things to all people has existed in more or less its current form for the last twenty-five years. In spite of a generally low (if good-humored) popular image of librarians, the demands on them have been high.

Training as a means to prepare librarians for the future is critical, but the direction to follow, depending as it does on the future of the profession, remains unclear. One dramatic forecast issues from what is regarded as one of the more certain predictions of the future of librarianship. Costs for library collections are not sustainable, and the obvious answer to this problem is network organizations and shared collections. Just as the works themselves will be held in common among many member institutions, the cataloging of records will be as well. Thus, there will be no need for local technical services, which will disappear—or be absorbed into the systems department (Saunders 1999, 6)! Accordingly, some have called for increased technical training for librarians to allow them to cooperate more with systems and keep up with the exponential advance in information technology. Others suggest that the role of technology in librarianship is overstated, and that the wholesale adoption of it at the expense of traditional skills is merely a faster way to make libraries extinct (Gorman 2003, 2, 40).

Some argue that in the highly competitive environment of the foreseeable future, librarians will also need business skills to market themselves, manage their operation, assess themselves, and sell their worth to university administration. Others, however, counter that the business model is fundamentally misapplied to an academic environment (Stoffle

et al. 2003, 368). Not only will it fail to do justice to the values of education and to the special environment of academia, but it may fail even in
financial terms.

In practical terms of library education, the issues sort into the basic
division between core courses and electives (Budd 2005, 249; Keys 1999,
171; Lynch and Smith 2001, 409). Should library schools radically change
their curricula? Or as Michael Gorman argues, should schools make sure
that all graduates have basic skills in reference, instruction, collection development, and cataloging, with the option to pursue further specialized
training on their own (Gorman 2003, 2, 10)? In other words, why sacri-
fice the defining center for the periphery? To address this question, faculty
were interviewed at two library science programs attached to two of our
case studies: UHM and Illinois. Andrew Wertheimer, chair of the Library and Information Science Program at UHM, describes that program as basically traditional, with a grounding in reference, cataloging,
and collection management, yet also unique in belonging to a computer
science department, which gives the students access to a wide variety of
courses (Wertheimer 2012). Students are required to take just two technology courses. "We require everyone to be abacus-friendly . . . Just kid-
ding," Wertheimer says. But all courses are current with technology, and
syllabi identify technologies relevant to their subject areas. In addition,
Wertheimer prepares his students for the future with its unknown technologies. "As a professional, you can't just go and say, 'I'm sorry, I didn't
learn this in school.' You have to be adaptable. That's throughout the curriculum that we emphasize all these things."

Linda Smith, Associate Dean for Academic Programs at the Graduate School of Library and Information Science (GSLIS) at Illinois, states
that one way to prepare students for the future of academic librarianship
is a course on trends in higher education so that they can understand the
context in which their library operates (L. Smith 2012). At the moment,
she says, GSLIS has invested in the developing field of data and digital
content management with specializations for students in data curation,
data analytics, and digital libraries. Terry Weech, an associate professor at
GSLIS, notes an irony here. "I've heard the term 'revenge of the catalogers'
because after all these years of really getting no respect from the public
services people, they eventually get the upper hand and are getting more
of the grant funds and more of the attention" (Weech 2012). But Weech
also notes that a basic uncertainty hangs over any attempt to predict the
future. "We can't even get hard information on where the majority of our
graduates end up, so it's hard to tell which kinds of training are getting

picked up." Even the common perception of the need for librarians is less certain than it seems. "It appears at one point some years back [the federal government] went through all the library standards for personnel . . . and they looked at a formula for the numbers of librarians needed to meet the standards. . . . It was all empirical, no research base." He noted that it was his understanding that the original numbers listed in the standards as the number of librarians needed to meet the standards were arrived at by a committee sitting around a room and making up the numbers they thought would be appropriate, more like a wish list than numbers arrived at after appropriate research. As the current chair of the Library Theory and Research Section of the International Federation of Library Associations and Institutions (IFLA), Weech also observed that the international interest in indigenous librarianship could be a possible new direction for librarians that does not rely on technology. It is a very worthy undertaking, he notes, but the degree of specialization imposes significant restrictions on the number of jobs. "I'm very conservative in looking at what we in professional education can do to provide students who've paid good money to get their degree. And I think it's fine if one wants to dedicate himself or herself to indigenous populations or provide access to or protection of indigenous knowledge. But there are not a lot of jobs in those areas" (Weech 2012).

Training is an issue for employed librarians as well. There has been a call for succession planning to blunt the impact of retirements and the loss of institutional knowledge as well as cross-training among various positions (Saunders 1999, 5; Scherrei 1997, 236). Some have also wondered at the value for librarians of pursuing secondary subject degrees or pure subject research as part of their positions. The desire for extra training is reflected in an increased demand for second master's degrees in job advertisements (Budd 2005, 252; Gromatzky 2002, 3, 4). The desire for extra certification also speaks to a much older desire of librarians to achieve equivalence to faculty; this movement crystallized in the 1960s but probably reaches back to the emergence of subject specialists and even to the birth of the profession in 1876. Yet Deborah Grimes has produced a study indicating that both instructional faculty and university administrators have little interest in librarians achieving outside degrees:

> Seen in this light, faculty status measured by teaching departmental criteria is a mantle that does not fit academic librarians and does not provide them with any power: The emperor is wearing no clothes. A struggle for faculty status based on

teaching faculty criteria depends, therefore, on nonindicators
of library centrality and probably is a waste of valuable time
and effort. (Grimes 1998, 99; see also Budd 2005, 268)

Thus in the area of library personnel, the fundamental choices facing librarianship remain: to reinvent ourselves, to blend the past and present,
or to perpetuate enduring principles of the profession in new forms.

CHAPTER FOUR

::

Technology

Technology in librarianship today is associated with computerized devices powered by electricity that have new capabilities and appear at an increasing rate. However, if the notion of technology is expanded to include all the different means of transmitting knowledge, then technology goes back to the beginnings of librarianship, and in all that time, libraries promoted technology rather than tried to catch up to it, as seems to be the case today. Language is often identified as the most significant invention of human beings and is bound up with the very definition of humanity. The earliest civilization in Mesopotamia is known for its distinctive writing system, recorded on clay tablets which were kept in libraries. The invention of the book in the medieval period was another powerful tool for information storage, preservation, and access (even if these books were often chained in place).

The arrival of Melvil Dewey upon the scene at Columbia continued the trend of promoting technology at libraries. He ensured that the library had the most recent equipment, such as the newly invented typewriter. For making copies, he preferred Thomas Edison's electric pen, a device which never gained popularity (Wiegand 1996, 50). With the growth of collections in the twentieth century, the card catalog—now an icon of a bygone era—played a radical role. The rapid increase in collections made it prohibitively expensive to update the book catalogs that had sufficed for more leisurely collection growth. An intense debate, now forgotten, pitted the merits of the new card catalog against the traditional approach (Schabas 1976, 209), a debate that in some ways foreshadowed the current arguments over the merits of print and online formats. In the event, the book catalog was pushed aside and the card catalog prevailed.

By allowing records to be, inserted, removed, altered, and re-sorted, the card catalog proved to be more flexible and economical. The card catalog was the HyperCard system (a precursor of the World Wide Web) of its time (Hamlin 1981, 35, 202; Wiegand 1996, 205).

In the interwar period, photographic technology had applications for libraries in the form of microfilm/fiche and microcards (Hamlin 1981, 212). By reducing text, these technologies aspired to address the rapid growth of library collections. Microcards sought to make the card catalog equivalent to the whole library by reproducing a text onto its index card (Rothstein 1976, 86). Print photocopies would follow shortly afterwards with the Xerox company. Yet while these technologies made significant impacts on collections, they did not have the transformative effects that were hoped for. In part, photographic technology would be overshadowed by advances in computer technology that accelerated during the Second World War (Gambee and Gambee 1976, 177). One outcome was the MARC record, developed in the 1960s. This invention brought card cataloging to its pinnacle and then displaced it (Gorman 2003, 12). With individual electronic records for items, it became possible to create Integrated Library Systems (ILS), fusing records for cataloging, circulation, and ILL into a single database system. The increased efficiency helped to keep pace with rapidly expanding collections and the growth of library services in the postwar era (Schabas 1976, 215). Computer technology also enabled online searching, thanks in part to the advent of Dialog, which facilitated the research of patrons. However, the command-line searching of Dialog with its elaborate rules (impenetrable to some library students), combined with the pressure of paying for time, made this service inaccessible to patrons. It did not give any indication of what was to come.

The Information Revolution, a complex phenomenon that includes the rise of the World Wide Web, e-mail technology, and other electronic resources, together with the growth of personal computers, is a departure from what came before by any reckoning. Patrons could now search for resources on their own without going to a specific location and mastering the rules of catalogs, indexes, and classification systems. Faced with the Internet and all it entails, libraries have formulated a complex response. Part of it consists of showing how libraries are different from the Internet and offer more even than their increasingly online collections. Rather than mere keepers of knowledge, librarians have cast themselves as guides who can lead patrons to the sources they need in the vast landscape of information (Grimes 1998, 118; Burke 2008, 275). Much of this guidance takes the form of critical evaluation of sources to determine which are relevant and credible among the many that can be summoned with the touch of a button. The guidance function is encapsulated in the concept of "information literacy." Traditionalists such as Gorman decry a concept that they consider useless and distracting from the core functions of libraries (Gorman 2003, 40). Yet, philosophically, information literacy goes back to the roots of the profession and Cutler's vision of a trained sensibility for the use of resources rather than just their retrieval. Efforts in library instruction will be discussed at more length in chapter 7, "Campus Roles."

While differentiating themselves from the Internet on one hand, libraries are also incorporating its technology on the other. One goal is to improve search interfaces. While librarians were laboriously trying to teach students the meaning of Boolean operators, wildcard searches, proximity operators, and nested statements, Google was setting the Internet on its head with a single search box, amidst a blank page, where one could input natural-language searches. Google's success speaks for itself. Accordingly, library catalog interfaces have become simpler by, for example, dispensing with Boolean operators. Some libraries have created interfaces that approach Google's in their simplicity. Displays of results replace detailed records and cloud-based, visually prominent "recommendations" replace subject terms.

While emulating the simplicity of sites like Google, libraries have also sought to borrow the Internet's ubiquitous availability. The Internet can be accessed at home, at specialized "cafés," and with laptops from bookstores. This reach has expanded further with tablets and smartphones, which are essentially miniaturized workstations. One can get online from virtually anywhere, even, as witnessed at UCD (the biking capital of America), while riding a bike. . . . Libraries have reached out to this new wave of "small mobile devices" by redesigning web pages and resources so that they can be accessed by this technology. The usage levels of mobile technology remain to be assessed, although the hopes of one political science professor that students will listen to his podcasts on the beach seem optimistic (Johnson et al. 2010, 10). The library has sought to project itself outward to patrons with technology in other ways. The aforementioned chat reference is one such way. Libraries have also entered into social media, with blogs mounted on library websites and through Facebook, YouTube, and the virtual world of Second Life (Maness 2006, 6).

Technology is expected to continue to grow at exponential rates, and if that proves true, particular technologies at this writing will pass away; the "killer app" is few and far between. Of greater importance is the audience that these technologies are designed to reach, and a good deal of research has been produced to understand the user populations of libraries (Rettig 2002, 17, 19, 20; Booth 2009, i). Pervading the results is a sense that individuals who grew up with the Information Revolution have fundamentally different outlooks and behavior patterns than others. Accordingly, there is a basic division between "digital natives," who grew up with the Internet, and "digital immigrants," who did not. Characteristics of the natives include multitasking behavior, high expectations of speed and convenience, casual attitudes toward schedules and relatively porous boundaries between work and play, an underdeveloped critical sense, and a confidence with technology. The literature is extensive (Booth 2009, 19). Yet rigid patterns tend to break down as one investigates more closely. For example, digital immigrants in some ways make more active use of certain advanced library technologies than digital natives. And one persistent result is that the actual skill level of digital natives tends to be significantly lower than their own perceptions of it (Chowdhury 2001, 275; Seiden 1997, 223; Booth 2009, 93; Weiler 2005, 50). Exactly how successful libraries will be in their efforts at outreach remains to be seen. But whatever form this engagement takes will depend on an accurate assessment of the user population. As libraries balance the need for trained guidance of these users with demands for increased technical efficiency, the tension between Cutler and Dewey will continue.

CHAPTER FIVE

::

Collections

Yet another of Thompson's permanent principles is that library collections must always grow (Thompson 1977, 210). This has not been evident through much of history, with the destruction that has overtaken collections in various forms. The greatest library in history, storehouse for the collected knowledge of the ancient world, in Alexandria, Egypt, was burned several times in its history, finally succumbing in AD 391. Libraries in the West continued the struggle, and in colonial America, despite extensive precautions against fire, library collections were all too often lost. A lack of copying technology together with a backward-looking education system focused on ancient knowledge further constrained the collection. Umberto Eco's novel *The Name of the Rose*, in which medieval monks poison the pages of books to prevent their theft, is no doubt an exaggeration, but the very existence of this story speaks to attitudes generated by the past (Eco 1983). This siege mentality changed with the modernization of libraries, which consisted of imitating German universities. But in contrast to the German seminar system, which sought specialized collections, American libraries acquired everything they could lay their hands on (Rothstein 1976, 81).

In part, the motive derived from a wholehearted embrace of the research model. Libraries sought to preserve information for all time but had no way of knowing which materials would be valuable for future researchers. The only remedy was to collect everything (Hamlin 1981, 93; Rothstein 1976, 84). Undoubtedly, libraries also partook in the entrepreneurial expansion of the country, which drove the funding of libraries and which was oriented toward quantitative results. Universities benefited by such policies as scholars, eager to advance themselves, sought out the largest collections with which to work. The growth of collections also drove the technology of the card catalog and was ultimately behind the emerging discipline of technical services (Rothstein 1976, 82). Specialists were needed for the many aspects of managing a collection, which included cataloging the material, circulating it, and preserving it.

But in the very flush of growth, libraries came to an unavoidable realization. Studies showed that libraries under a wide variety of circumstances double their collection size every sixteen years—an exponential rate (Budd 2005, 27).

$C = C_0 2^{(t/16)}$ where C is collection size, C_0 is the initial collection, and t is time in years.

With this growth rate, increased funding for library collections only allowed libraries to maintain their coverage of available materials; like Alice in Wonderland, the harder the libraries ran, the more they stayed in place or even moved backwards (Rothstein 1976, 93). Science shows that exponential growth rates are unsustainable in any environment. In the context of libraries, cost is one limiter. No library can sustain the cost of a collection that grows exponentially. Another limiter is space. In the 1940s, a calculation showed that at its then current growth rate, the Yale University Library by the year 2040 would house 200 million books requiring eight acres of land for storage (Rider 1944, 12). The only truly practical solution for libraries was to form cooperative networks to share resources. This practice had appeared at the beginning of modern librarianship. Samuel Green, the father of reference for public libraries, called for libraries to borrow books that they did not have from other libraries. Dewey instituted a similar practice at Columbia (Hamlin 1981, 182, 184, 185). Interlibrary loan (ILL) allowed libraries to share both space and funds to support collections that each one could not possess individually.

ILL continued to grow more robust in the early twentieth century and was formalized by the Farmington Plan in the late 1940s (Hamlin 1981, 54). Library networks promised to solve other problems related to the growth of collections (Calter, Shore, and Williford 2010, 2). The labor-intensive cataloging of items represented another form of duplication among libraries, with implications for time and expense that could be significantly attenuated through networks. Other forms of cooperation followed, including shared acquisitions. To these ends, the Center for Research Libraries and the Ohio College Library Center (OCLC) were created after World War II (Rothstein 1976, 97). Electronic information storage, which was not far behind, would contribute to shared collections by reducing space requirements relative to print and allowing for remote access.

The economic crisis of 2008, however, has brought into focus the implications of new technologies, both positive and negative, for collections. The limits to exponential growth, anticipated for so long, are being reached now, and libraries are running out of space for print materials. Offsite storage and compact shelving merely postpone the problem of limited space for print collections and not for long. In the context of this crisis, John Wilkin, former executive director of the HathiTrust, a digital repository, and now Dean of Libraries and University Librarian at Illinois, writes of how little we know about the vast trove of library collections, a condition which he describes as "bibliographic indeterminacy":

> We know that there are more than 1 billion volumes being stored in North American academic libraries. We don't know, however, how many unique instances or manifestations there are. My hunch, based on the results of collection overlap analysis in HathiTrust, is that it's unlikely to be more than 50 million unique instances, which in turn should lead us to conclude that there's considerable duplication. That duplication is made more pressing when we take into account the fact that large portions of our collections go unused for decades. (Wilkin 2012)

Studies show that 80 percent of library print collections are not used, and that if an item is not checked out shortly after acquisition (when it can gain recognition and word-of-mouth publicity), its chances of ever being used drop precipitously (Knieval, Wicht, and Connaway 2006; O'Neill and Gammon 2009). So the giant, burdensome collections being maintained at such expense are not even being used! Such a dramatic problem has called forth dramatic solutions. Daniel Greenstein, former Vice Provost for Academic Planning and Programs at the University of California, voiced an idea that has surfaced repeatedly (Kolowich 2009). The library of the future, he claimed, will consist of large shared collections stored remotely. As much as possible, these collections will be digitized for easy storage and retrieval. Libraries, as we know them, will shrink to distribution points for the shared collections with perhaps some basic services for reference. Special collections will grow to make up the core of individual libraries, which is to say materials of primarily local interest. Such a transformation would solve all the problems of space and cost facing libraries in a stroke. In effect, the collection would become the determining characteristic of libraries. This was largely true for much of history, but rather than confirming libraries in their traditional mission, the new plan would change libraries as we know them (Bennett 2009, 187).

Since the new centralized vision relies so heavily on electronic storage, it is appropriate to examine this technology in more depth. There are large apparent advantages. This medium radically extends the miniaturization that has driven much technological development. Where microcards could reduce the text of a book onto its catalog card, CD-ROMs of comparable size could store vastly more—virtually whole libraries, and the material could be retrieved with much greater convenience than with the cumbersome old readers of microcards and microfiche. These advantages have grown exponentially with online storage. Yet there are powerful disadvantages and complications as well.

While electronic journals have been embraced, electronic books have lagged considerably. In part this has to do with practical matters related to their greater length. Many readers have found that the sustained reading that one typically does for books is more difficult online. The eye blinks far less frequently while reading, and in this condition, it is exposed to the direct light of computer screens, which is much more tiring for eyes than the reflected light from book pages (Sheedy 2007). Screen lighting technology has improved but still cannot duplicate the ease of print reading. A study at Princeton University also found that readers disliked using e-books because they could not write marginal comments on the text (although one would hope that the same applies to print books from the library collection) (Lee 2009). E-books also struggle with incompatible technologies for storing and reading content. The entrepreneurial energy that has driven information technology has spawned a variety of independent businesses whose products do not interconnect (Titangos and Jan 2007, 9; Seaman 2005, 56). Optimists point to the relative success of Amazon's Kindle and growing e-book sales in general to predict that the technological problems will be solved in time, but that time has not arrived yet. One of the library's two traditional formats is severely restricted.

There are also misgivings about whether electronic storage is cheaper, as it has been perceived to be. The preference for using print for sustained reading implies that at some point, most electronic articles, as well as electronic books, will be printed out. And by some calculations, the process of printing and reprinting electronic texts will consume more paper and ink than the print industry (Crawford and Gorman 1995, 96; MacWhinnie 2003, 242; Brown and Calia-Lotz 2005, 87). As another consideration, the success of electronic journals comes at a cost that has increased faster than for any other category of material (Budd 2005, 174; McGuigan 2004, 13). Prices have outpaced inflation and production costs and appear to some to be driven by the whims of database vendors. To be fair, there are also costs for selecting the journals, digitizing their contents (especially print-only back issues), and uploading them to databases, as well as for marketing the databases. After all this labor has been added to the price of the content, the prospect for saving costs relative to print is less promising.

Even consortia, an aspect of future collection-building designed to reduce prices, have proven more complicated than initially predicted. Subscription bundles purchased by consortia provide its smaller member libraries access to resources that they could not otherwise afford (Keys 1999, 179). But does this really save money for libraries? Smaller libraries find that their consortial dues are applied to titles that they do not need but cannot delete from the total package (Budd 2005, 186). The package deal starts to look like a form of exploitation by vendors. Large libraries, for their part, wonder if the library consortia benefit them either. Given the unequal size of member libraries, the larger support the smaller, and the flow of resources is in one direction (Rothstein 1976, 101). As a means of survival, libraries have resorted to "consortium shopping," juggling consortia memberships and different pricing details until the last minute (Keys 1999, 180). This plays hell with vendors, who, unable to decide on prices that are viable for them, are forced ultimately to raise prices to prevent shortfall. A related confusion about cost extends to the sharing of print resources in ILL. Gorman observes that after borrowing a book twice through ILL, it would be cheaper for a library to buy a copy for itself (Crawford and Gorman 1995, 152). This would seem to set severe limits on the potential for ILL to reduce costs. Generally, the cooperation among libraries that was intended for mutual benefit seems to have generated mistrust, chaos, and greater expense.

Intertwined issues of cost and control also impinge on preservation. Libraries have always collected human knowledge for all time. While technology has improved and the threat of unpredictable mass violence and destruction has diminished from earlier times, new dangers have arisen. The purchase of electronic materials by subscription is temporary. As libraries rely more and more on this form of material, the more vulnerable they become to vendors or some outside agency discontinuing access for any number of reasons (Keys 1999, 171). Even when libraries are success-fully subscribed, this underlying dependence implies that libraries have *already* ceded their stewardship of material for the future. There are also technological problems that are less malevolent but ultimately just as damaging. Among the many different and competing forms of technology in use, some will no doubt fall out of use in the future. If electronic storage technologies were to disappear, their materials would be lost as surely as if they had been destroyed by fire and sword. The humble book has an unsurpassed record for preservation through the centuries, and this fact alone could offset economic factors in retaining this format.

Books and print media, however, pose problems of their own for preservation. Observers have noted that in a shared collection, the safety of a book is inversely proportional to its access (Crawford and Gorman 1995, 131). Given a limited number of copies for a set of users, liberal loan policies as envisioned for shared collections will expose materials to risk and damage. And as we have just seen, using ILL beyond a certain point will eliminate the savings that a shared collection is supposed to gain. At another extreme, the protection of a few copies with walls of reg-ulations will make the work unavailable and, from the point of view of borrowers, as good as destroyed. How many copies should be preserved? A rigorous mathematical derivation proves daunting (Yano, Shen, and Chan 2008). And who is to decide where they will be stored and the pol-icies for lending them? The dimensions of the political problems are vast. They form one basis for a counter-movement among librarians who argue that the vision of shared collections will not do. Robust local collections are necessary for libraries to respond adequately to their universities and other populations that they serve. Among the seven trends considered here, the future form of collections is perhaps the pivot that will most de-termine the development of libraries.

CHAPTER SIX

::

Buildings

The facilities that have housed library collections through history are a story in their own right. According to Thompson, they have been associated from the very beginning with wealth and power (Thompson 1977, 64; Neary 2011). In ancient times, libraries were often housed in temples and borrowed their impressive architecture. Libraries thus served a dual purpose of storing collections and symbolizing their significance. With the passing of the ancient world went also the vast sprawling design of libraries open to all. Libraries of the medieval period were small, owing to a scarcity of books. Housed amidst unstable and violent societies, the materials tended to be well protected, as suggested by the forbidding Gothic architecture of some university libraries (Thompson 1977, 184). Eco's imagined medieval library, designed as a labyrinth to trap and destroy thieves (lest they escape the poisoned pages), evokes some of this history.

The college libraries of colonial America and the early republic, continuing as they did the medieval educational traditions, were humble affairs. When libraries were granted even a single room (as opposed to a cabinet), it was often placed above the chapel or at some out-of-the-way location (Budd 2005, 18; Hamlin 1981, 27, 149, 152). Collections were meager enough that they could be stored by lining the walls. While Melvil Dewey did not contribute to external architecture, he did, as part of his campaign to encourage reading and library use, introduce change to library interiors. He increased the use of natural lighting through windows. Carpets were laid down to dampen noise, retain warmth, and provide a more comfortable, inviting environment. Dewey also equipped book carts with rubber wheels and his staff with soft-soled shoes to minimize noise. Ice water was provided for the refreshment of readers. And above all,

Dewey exerted his relentless vigilance in keeping the library clean. He had printed up a set of cards which said, "I picked up these pieces in the hall and infer that you threw them on the floor. My time and that of my assistants is too valuable for this work. Still we prefer to do it rather than have the building so disfigured." It was no doubt a chilling experience for patrons who received such a card (which substituted for a spoken admonition, to reduce noise). As one observer said, "He thinks of all the details . . . [he] even teaches the sub-janitors how to dust books properly" (Wiegand 1996, 84, 192).

The Boston Public Library, the original modern library in America, provided a basic floor plan (in the McKim Building, which opened in 1895) that became a model for other libraries both public and academic (Hamlin 1981, 155). The patron entered a front door then proceeded up a staircase to the second floor, where a reference desk was located and from where he or she could enter the book stacks. As collection sizes increased, books extended out from the walls in transverse or radial stacks, and some even climbed the walls to a considerable height that was reached by ladder (Thompson 1977, 198; Kaser 1997, 6–7). After a certain point, whole wings were devoted to books, extending the basic pattern of the Boston Public Library. Stacks typically occupied wings to either side of a central reading area, containing a reference desk. In some cases, libraries assumed a T shape, with stacks extending behind the building perpendicular to the line formed by the central element and its two wings (Kaser 1997, 99; Rogers 1976, 226). The spirit of the mission behind the Boston Public Library expressed itself in monumentalism, a recurrent theme in library buildings that recalled earlier ages when libraries had represented authority and power. Typical features included imposing outer facades, large internal spaces and staircases, and a décor both inside and out reminiscent of palaces or temples (Hamlin 1981, 156; Thompson 1977, 187; Webb 2000b, 9).

New library buildings both public and academic proliferated throughout the nation at the turn of the twentieth century, much of them through the single-handed philanthropy of Andrew Carnegie. In keeping with Carnegie's utilitarian orientation, many of these buildings reflected an alternative architecture of form follows function, and this theme was to contrast with monumentalism down through the years (Hamlin 1981, 156; Kaser 1997, 63). In some cases, form was obligated to follow function because of practical demands. As collection size skyrocketed, buildings came to resemble warehouses whose main function was to store the collection. Even today, some claim that the simple box remains the ideal structure for libraries (Edwards 2000, 148). To maximize this space, a new form of storage had been invented in the early twentieth century consisting of stacks of metal shelves that could be hooked together to fill available space (Hamlin 1981, 152; Kaser 1997, 85; Rogers 1976, 224). Some buildings became solid with books as they subdivided their interiors into floors filled with such stacks. In order to transmit light while at the same time protecting privacy (especially for women), the mezzanine flooring was designed to be translucent. Patrons in the midst of the cloudy vista of shelves going in all directions may well have had the sensation of floating among books (Rogers 1976, 232).

At the same time, however, the development of specialized departmental libraries was carving out enclaves among the mass of books with dedicated collections and reference desks for subject experts. A related movement sought to improve the comfort of readers and facilitate use of the collection. Continual efforts were made to increase lighting and provide reading spaces equipped with suitable desks and chairs. In some cases, stack height was reduced to provide a more open atmosphere.

A third and final major phase of library architecture appeared after the Second World War and transformed libraries and society as a whole. Inspired by the many technological innovations of the war, planners introduced "modular libraries" (Hamlin 1981, 160, 162, 165; Thompson 1977, 201; Kaser 1997, 107). As before, the building plan was simple; each floor plan was made identical to the others. The modularity consisted of the use of partitions, furniture, and other means available to repurpose and rearrange space without significant renovation. The library was built to accommodate change as a matter of principle. The more modern designs aimed at greater convenience for the users. Reading spaces became lounges with comfortable furniture. And as personal computers appeared, they were used to equip labs for instruction and individual research. In spite of the steady downward trajectory of funding since the 1970s, new construction has continued in waves to suit the needs of individual campuses. There was a notable burst of building in the 1990s that hearkened back to the monumentalism of earlier times (Webb 2000b, 13; Rudin 2008, 56; Loder 2010, 349). Modernization was also a big theme for this wave of libraries, which included large computer labs and clusters of workstations throughout the building, computer-driven projectors and interactive whiteboards for instruction, and large numbers of outlets for people to plug in their own laptops. Some libraries loaned out laptops. Extensive accommodation was made for study areas, including rooms suitable for the team projects that were gaining vogue in higher education.

The economic crisis of 2008 brought expansion to a halt, putting into sharp focus the issues related to library buildings. As mentioned in the discussion of collections, libraries, even after factoring in remote storage facilities and compact shelving, are running out of space for print collections (Gayton 2008, 64; Shill and Tonner 2003, 453). Also, just as reference services have been waning, the gate counts at library buildings appear to be declining, too. Figures of 20 and 32 percent reduction over the last twenty years appear in the literature (Gayton 2008, 61; Shill and Tonner 2003, 432). Presumably the Internet and related electronic library resources, which have allowed patrons to bypass traditional reference service, have also enabled them to avoid using the library building altogether. Given the massive costs of maintaining large buildings that are not even being used, why continue to operate them? Indeed, Greenstein's call for shared collections implied a radical reduction in the physical plant of libraries. Ironically, within a decade of the renaissance in library buildings, powerful reasons emerged to shut them down. This goal has been pursued in various ways.

Some libraries have chosen to reduce hours, in many cases tailoring them around trends of usage. Other libraries have sought to close their branches, consolidating them together on a campus. Still others have sought to lease out library space to other campus departments to get them to share the cost of maintaining the space. These libraries began looking to form partnerships that would not only remain true to the library's mission but in some cases actually provide new and improved services. In addition to academic departments, candidates for new occupants of library buildings have included counseling and tutoring services, computing services, and library administration (Rudin 2008, 59; Tooey 2010, 42).

Since money has become such a driving factor, some creative ideas have sought to deploy library building space to generate revenue. One practice is to get individuals or organizations to donate plaques in the building for a fee. Donors can also purchase various pieces of equipment such as desks, furniture, benches, cabinets, or whole rooms. (Some libraries have even opened the collection itself to donors, through programs which allow names to be added to a "bookplate" on the initial page of a book.) Another trend is the library café. This represents a radical break with tradition, in which librarians have fought a running battle with patrons to block food and drink from libraries. Such refreshments, like patron noise, were deemed inimical to the library environment, and preservationists, alarmed at the notion of spilled drinks, crumbs, and crawling bugs, have considered them a threat to the collection itself. One can only wonder at Dewey's response to eaters and drinkers. However, the very vigor of the enemy suggested a deep connection between snacking and studying. An entire new industry of mega-bookstores such as Barnes & Noble has installed lounges and cafés, and Starbucks, a nominal coffeehouse, has reinvented itself by creating lounge space where one can read and connect to the Internet while enjoying coffee. In fact, the historical tradition of cafés as intellectual centers has been reinvigorated by Internet access (Rudin 2008, 58; Massie 1980, 205). Beset by competitors in the provision of information, the library can no longer afford to forbid food and drink based on fear alone (well-founded or not). There is a certain logic, therefore, to libraries incorporating their own cafés. These services aim to attract and retain users as well as generate new income.

Library buildings themselves offer another commodity with their large spaces and the impressive decors of monumentalism. Libraries have considered renting space for campus functions, exhibits, and even for private functions such as weddings. And in another forward-looking use of the physical plant, libraries have sought to engage in sustainable or green technologies. This has economic implications. A common idea is to install solar panels on the roof to meet the library's energy needs. Other ideas include redesigns to make more use of natural lighting and dry or double flush toilets, all of which are regulated by LEED standards. (LEED is an acronym for Leadership in Environmental Energy and Design, a suite of rating systems designed by the U.S. Green Building Council.) With such initiatives, libraries hope both to save money and to involve themselves in issues of sustainability, which command increasing attention on university campuses (Loder 2010, 348).

In buildings as in other aspects of its service, libraries have sought not only to accommodate change but also to use it to move forward. Buildings now seek to provide study space for patrons as much as a storehouse for the collection (Hamlin 1981, 136). Scott Bennett has reformulated the history of library buildings around their purposes over time, and the latest and current mission is to encourage learning by their very design (Budd 2005, 155; Bennett 2009, 181). One simple, practical application of this idea is to offer a haven of quiet study, especially to undergraduates. Current news reports would seem to suggest that the alcoholism, violence, and intense sexual activity revealed in the wake of the murder of a member of the University of Virginia women's lacrosse team by her boyfriend constitutes normal campus behavior (see Winston and Schoenberg 2012). Another high-profile case at Rutgers University at about the same time, involving a student's use of a webcam to spy on a gay roommate's sexual encounter, confirms that privacy and quiet seclusion may be hard to come by on campus. Increasingly, libraries have stepped in to fill this need—for example, by providing twenty-four-hour study rooms, protected zones in time and space (Atlas, Wallace, and Fleet 2005, 316).

Others have observed that the trend toward interdisciplinary research has given library buildings a new significance. It is perhaps the only site on campus where members of different departments come into contact with each other during their work, and this proximity enables the crossing of boundaries and the creation of possibilities (Kranich 2001, 84). Libraries are seeking to capitalize on this phenomenon with a different type of space, called the Learning or Information Commons (Budd 2005, 153; Rudin 2008, 57, 58; Bennett 2009, 188).

Though the concept of a Learning Commons has been out for a while, an exact definition remains elusive. Perhaps that is to the point. The commons is not really designed for a specific function in the way that a reference desk answers questions, the circulation desk checks out items, and the ILL department borrows and loans. Rather, the Learning Commons is a space for creativity and interaction in the way of the fora and agora of the ancient world, the town commons of a later era, or the student debating societies of the nineteenth century (Bennett 2009, 189; Lippincott and Greenwell 2011, 1). The Learning Commons, therefore, is defined in terms of elements that can enhance creativity. To begin with, it is an attractive reading lounge. Surveys and focus groups of student library patrons consistently assign a high priority to "comfy" chairs and other furniture for study areas. But rather than being simply a form of indulgence, these features address some of the new learning behaviors of digital natives who engage in multitasking. As they come and go to the library café, for instance, students increasingly desire accommodations to socialize and interact with others as well as to reflect by themselves. Chairs, pillows, and tables of various sizes enable these various activities. Another defining feature of the commons is technology. Plans call for the latest technology in the form of interactive whiteboards, workstations with a full suite of software, full-service printers with color and scanning, and perhaps laptops available for loan (Gayton 2008, 62). This technology might be accompanied by roving staff who combine the skills of a reference librarian and information technology personnel. Such a space would combine improved reference, technology, and facility usage.

But even at the hypothetical stage, there are questions. Gayton claims that in reaching for a new sense of community, libraries will betray the communal atmosphere that they have had all along (Gayton 2008, 60;

Bennett 2009, 182). This exists in the quiet, studious environment associated with libraries all the way back to the days of medieval monasteries. Paradoxically, in the act of quiet reading, library patrons function at their cooperative and productive best. In contrast, the disorganized, social, and presumably noisier environment of the Learning Commons will destroy the old atmosphere and replace it with something hypothetical and untested. It is not easy to see how complaints about noise from angry patrons, which have always been a feature of libraries, will be handled in the new environment.

Assessment has been done on recent library buildings which incorporate new ideas—especially those having to do with more computer labs, additional outlets for laptops, and more and better-equipped study areas. The central question is whether the new buildings can reverse the decline in gate counts. The provisional answer is that gate counts are not tied to new buildings, but they do improve as a function of the modern features enumerated here (Gayton 2008, 64; Rudin 2008, 57; Shill and Tonner 2004, 127). These results promise hope for the future of library space.

A library's space stands in a certain opposition to its collection, which, in an age of networks and interlibrary sharing, seems to point toward the reduction of the physical plant. The bigger question is whether library buildings will continue their role as centers of power and, if so, what form this power will take. Rather than amassing print materials, it appears that the library of the future will provide an environment for creativity and inquiry.

⠶

Campus Roles

Such was the pace of growth of libraries after 1876 that, by 1900, the description of the library as the "heart of the university" was coined (Hamlin 1981, 50; Rothstein 1976, 80). This heart consisted of the massive, expanding collections that were the focus of librarianship and the buildings needed to house them. But just as the library rode to prominence on a tide of funding and collection growth, the reduction of both of these in the long decline of the 1970s forced a reconsideration of identity, and this was given further urgency with the rise of the Internet as a rival. With virtual information accessible from anywhere, in what sense can the library continue as the heart of the campus?

An alternative role for the library was actually some time in the making and developed from traditional functions. Implicit in the very concept of reference that was articulated in 1876 was a teaching role, which, as we have seen, formed a bone of contention between Dewey and Cutler. The issue was not whether to teach but how (Hamlin 1981, 144). The question of teaching grew steadily with the growth of collections and the reference service that grew to keep pace with it, culminating in the triage network of specialists. To remove the burden of simple, repetitive questions, formalized instruction was instituted with the growth of Bibliographic Instruction (BI) as a separate field in the post-war era (Burke 2008, 271). Rather than having reference service repeat the same information to individuals, instruction staff could speak once to an assembled group. As the name implies, the content of BI was concerned with the print collection: the use of the card (then online) catalog, call numbers, and various print indexes and reference tools.

With the arrival of the Internet and the World Wide Web, BI was positioned to change from an ancillary service to a more central role, redefining librarianship (Rader 1999, 213; Cardina and Wicks 2004, 134). With its massive content, advanced technology, and sheer strangeness, this new era brought with it a good deal of confusion as well as possibility. Library instruction assumed a new importance in leading patrons through the new environment; in the process, the role of the library was redefined as a guide to knowledge. If this role is central to a new identity, then instruction, which engages users in large numbers, is its most visible manifestation. It is no accident that instruction departments are commonly assigned the role of outreach (Cardina and Wicks 2004, 134).

Library instruction has defined its purpose around a new theory of literacy, a broad movement in education. Whereas *literacy* is commonly defined as the functional ability to read and write, *information literacy* generalizes the concept. Before users can gain access to the texts they should read, they need to identify and locate these texts—a challenge determined by the questions that the researcher wants to answer. So information literacy is conceived of as a process. First the researcher needs to form a proper set of questions. Then he or she needs to select the correct tool and learn to use it properly. Normally, this entails choosing the correct database among the many that might be available and then taking advantage of its particular interface to search its voluminous contents. This available information, however, does little good unless the researcher is able to understand it and then apply some critical thinking skills to evaluate it against the research goals; here, librarianship participates in the most basic goals of higher education. Having absorbed and digested the material, the researcher completes the process through an act of production, which raises additional challenges. The researcher must understand how to use the information ethically. This includes practical considerations of copyright and privacy as well as more abstract issues of using the information in a principled way. Some versions of information literacy define the concept to include the production of new knowledge using technologies such as spreadsheets, PowerPoint, visualization software, citation management applications, and word processors. The Association of College and Research Libraries formalized the concept of information literacy with the publication of standards accompanied by an exhaustive list of practices and indicators (Association of American Colleges and Universities 2000).

To teach information literacy, instruction programs have imagined a common progression. Incoming students receive a basic orientation to the library building and services that generally includes a physical tour.

Then, students receive introductory training to the library's collection through an instruction session commonly held in first-year seminars and introductory writing classes. For more advanced classes, students receive further instruction on more specialized tools. Yet regardless of how high the level of instruction, such teaching is hampered by the format of the "one-shot" session, even when a librarian is fortunate enough to get two of them in a term. There is no opportunity to review and reinforce material, to get to know the students, to develop advanced topics, or to interact with students about their written work. Studies indicate that students retain distressingly little from these isolated sessions. According to Michael Atlas, for example, "My own experience . . . is that during 'live' information literacy sessions held in new computer labs, students focus on whatever is on the screen (sport scores, instant messages, sometimes even the lesson), rather than what the real-live librarian in front of them is trying to convey to the class" (Atlas, Wallace, and Fleet 2005, 315). The hope was that one-shot sessions would be a transition state toward credit courses in information literacy, where students would study the subject over the course of a term. Such a course would also have a salutary effect on the quest of librarians for faculty status. However, the march of library instruction and information literacy appears to have stalled. While library credit courses do exist, they have not appeared in significant numbers. In part, this is because of the general strain on resources imposed by budget cuts in the wake of the recent financial crisis. There is no great willingness to devote resources to a new type of course from libraries at a time when established courses are being cancelled from lack of funding. Also, reduced numbers of faculty, assigned larger numbers of students, are jealous of their time. While they typically appreciate one-shot sessions, they are loath to dedicate more time to libraries in preference to their own material. And it may be that a sense of professional hierarchy still applies in not seeing library training as deserving of equivalent attention with traditional course content. The one-shot session has proven to be an intractable barrier. And given that Dewey himself ran a credit course in librarianship and that these have appeared occasionally since then, it appears that libraries are not breaking such new ground after all (Hamlin 1981, 57).

In response, instruction librarians along with other parts of the profession have exhibited considerable energy and creativity in making themselves relevant. Instruction labs, which are typically equipped with workstations and projectors, see a steady flow of new technologies. Interactive whiteboards (Smart Boards) record writing that can be saved, printed, or e-mailed. Clickers allow instant class feedback to the instructor and engage the students (Bhavnagri and Bielat 2005, 125). Perhaps a new technology will make the difference. And these tools are being used within new instructional practices derived from recent theories about the importance of discussion, group work, hands-on practice, and openness to a variety of learning styles (MacWhinnie 2003, 242; Kaser 1997, 123). Outside the classroom, instruction has mimicked reference in seeking out patrons. This is done asynchronously through remote teaching devices such as tutorials and iPod tours that students can access at any time.

Another set of strategies comes under one sense of the term "embedding," where librarians seek to blend into the structure of a course. This approach makes no extra demands on class time while giving librarians more sustained contact with the class. Embedding can take the form of participating on an instructor's courseware and "lurking" on discussion boards or cooperating more on the design and evaluation of assignments. In other cases, librarians visit classrooms to observe or give guest talks. This requires an unusual level of cooperation between faculty and librarians and high motivation (and often extra funding). An intriguing study has explored the limits of what might be possible (Bowler and Street 2008). Over several courses, a library and faculty member employed different degrees of cooperation. Five levels defined a range from least involvement, with librarians merely helping in the design of assignments, to total immersion, where librarians co-taught courses in the guise of instructional faculty. Student performance on coursework improved with increasing library involvement until the last stage: quality dropped when the librarians taught disguised as a faculty member compared to when the librarian co-taught while identified as a librarian. This is surprising, given the assumption that more is better with the goal of seamless involvement of the library in courses. Perhaps there is a limit to the quest of instruction librarians for more course hours and equivalent status to faculty who teach courses for credit. In fact, the results of the study suggest that the library is partly valued for its visibility as a library. Perhaps the way forward for librarians lies with a redefinition of mission and audience rather than a quest for more class time or specific pedagogies.

Distance learning is another frontier for the development of library instruction. It has become a major force in higher education that looks to continue growing. While the focus remains on the technology, the primary driver is economic. Schools can gain vast numbers of new students, their primary source of revenue, without supporting additional facilities for housing and teaching them (Budd 2005, 6). And the demands on faculty are comparatively low, since online education is conducive to mass teaching. Libraries, however, have not fared particularly well in this environment. Indeed, there does seem to be great promise. Information technology is becoming increasingly central to the mission of libraries, and it is much closer to their area of expertise than that of most faculty. Librarians should stand to gain a larger share of an increasingly larger pie. Consider, however, the interactions between faculty and students in a distance-learning environment. Chat and real-time video notwithstanding, the quality of interaction between an instructor and student cannot duplicate what happens in a traditional classroom, and it remains a struggle to impart the same amount of teaching to what is typically a much larger group. Factor in the instructional librarian's minimal presence in traditional classes, and it shrinks proportionally in an online environment to virtually nothing. It is perhaps worth mentioning here that one of Melvil Dewey's many initiatives in his whirlwind career at Columbia was remote instruction in the form of correspondence courses (Wiegand 1996, 150). In his mind, this program fit perfectly with his vision of librarianship as a form of education based on directed reading. Students would meet introductory requirements through a curriculum of reading and complete their education in person for the final year. However, the Board of Regents at Columbia drew the line at this idea, which compromised their notion of a university. Decades later, librarians find themselves facing a different kind of uncertainty over distance education.

Meanwhile, technology has raised some completely new opportunities. Instruction has been generally interpreted to apply to the classroom setting (real or virtual). However, this accounts in time for only a small part of education, which occurs largely outside the classroom. In fact, the German research model gave priority to individual research over classroom teaching, and research has become only more important with new technologies for producing, storing, and copying information. The pace of publication has increased exponentially along with the growth of collections (Budd 2005, 7). What if libraries could move beyond teaching altogether to intervene more directly in the research process itself? This is now possible with bibliographic management software. Established brands such as EndNote, RefWorks, Reference Manager, and ProCite have been supplemented with open-source versions such as Zotero and Mendeley, suggesting that this technology has found a niche. While originally designed to automate the storage, formatting, and retrieval of citations—essentially mechanical work—the technology has incorporated new functions to organize and manage information so as to engage users more deeply with the research process. In the process of teaching the software, librarians are placed as never before to participate in the act of research by working on the entire information literacy process in a way that is not bounded by walls or daily schedules. In doing so, librarians can have a positive influence on completion rates at both undergraduate and graduate levels, which, in a time of reduced budgets, are becoming increasingly critical (Oakleaf 2010, 32). Research, however, is a private, specialized activity; intervention will be slow and progress remains to be seen.

Information management enables another role for librarians that is new but which also strikes to the roots of the modern research university. As a professional activity, academic research requires a gatekeeping function to determine work that meets the necessary standards and work that does not. Thus was born the mechanism of peer review. The professoriate review new work, and approval is determined by key journals and academic presses for each field. But over time and with the appearance of information technology, this seemingly straightforward, internal process has produced unexpected effects that in many cases are harmful to the profession. As part of the fine print, scholars typically sign over all the rights to their work to scholarly publications in a way that surpasses what is required of commercial authors (Crawford and Gorman 1995, 161; McGuigan 2004, 16). These key publications, in turn, have become the focus of information distributors such as journal vendors who, operating from a business model, want to secure the best commodity for distribution. Indeed, their product of convenient access to prestigious publications has been hugely attractive and even game-changing for harried academic researchers.

But the very success of this product has led to monopolies, with all of their consequences. Vendors are free to raise prices, which they have proceeded to do. Thus, the profession's mechanism of peer review has been co-opted by business interests to bleed money from libraries and the universities that they represent. There are three players in this process, all of which have distinct functions. Scholars create knowledge. Vendors publish it. And libraries distribute it. However, what should be an equal and cooperative relationship based on the relative importance of the contribution has become altered so that scholars and libraries are at the mercy of vendors (Keys 1999, 173). This is highly ironic since the university, in the form of both scholars and libraries, sustains the industry in the first place.

Recent budget pressures have spurred efforts to redress the imbalance, and libraries are positioned to take a leading role. One immediate tool is to boycott the most expensive and offending vendors, such as the Nature Publishing Group, a step that was taken by the California Digital Library (CDL), which manages licenses for UC schools (see http://osc .universityofcalifornia.edu/npg/). Boycott requires the coordination of faculty members, since they depend on these products for their own research. Libraries, which distribute material to all academic disciplines, are well-positioned to do this. Yet ultimately, faculty must have an alternative to vendors for a boycott to stick. Here again, the library can play a role. This can take the form of providing technology for faculty to digitize and publish their work and make it available. The developing field of e-science (or e-research) is coalescing around the practices and technologies required to do this. Faculty and libraries would appear to have the tools to make themselves independent of vendors (Cardina and Wicks 2004, 135; Stoffle et al. 2003, 370; Brown and Calia-Lotz 2005, 85; Webb 2000a, 258).

Yet there are significant challenges too, and the outcome is not assured. There are many technological hurdles beyond the digitization of material. Vendors would argue that, in fact, they are not mere middlemen or opportunistic robber barons, fleecing commerce without contributing to it. Specialized expertise and expense are involved in selecting information, indexing it, mounting it on electronic platforms, distributing and marketing it, and performing other functions to ensure that the whole operation remains solvent. To threats of boycott and workarounds, one response of vendors is "go ahead and try . . ." (Hall 2005, 69, 70). A second and perhaps even greater barrier is cultural in nature. The peer-review model that is so basic to the research university is intrinsically hierarchical, as seen in the common phrase "publish or perish." Fundamentally, a work will be published or it will not. And among those which are, there is a fine hierarchy of value all the way to the very top. For faculty to set this aside and seek some alternative recognition for their work goes against their professional imperative to excel (Crawford and Gorman 1995, 68, 162; McGuigan 2004, 24). There are opportunities as well as significant hurdles for libraries as they seek to maintain their role as guides to learning and providers of information in a new environment.

CHAPTER EIGHT

::

Library Culture

The very concept of culture has come under intense scrutiny in recent times with the culture wars of the 1990s and the creation of cultural studies as an academic discipline. A common definition of culture is the sum total of a society's thoughts, actions, and very existence (French and Bell 1999, 30; Overall 2009, 180). But this definition is so broad as to have little practical value. Nevertheless, a subject that is so elusive may also by some reckonings be the most important factor in the future of libraries.

The material artifacts and the very collections of ancient libraries have been mostly lost, so their even more ephemeral cultures are irrecoverable. It is fair to say in more modern times that American college libraries prior to 1876 had a moribund and inert culture, as discussed earlier. But now, when libraries are sometimes accused of being traditional, backward-looking, and resistant to change, one loses sight of the fact that the founder of modern academic libraries, Melvil Dewey, although a cataloger—a role traditionally associated with standards and details—was innovative and aggressive to a fault (Edgar 1976, 308; Oakleaf 2010, 28; Maness 2006). Consumed by his moral vision and a degree of egotism, it was his practice to override every obstacle and person who stood in his way. He founded the basic institutions of librarianship, but as secretary to its governing bodies, he identified himself so totally with them that he felt entitled to move funds between different offices. His creative accounting became hopelessly confused and led to his ouster, a recurring theme in his long and active career. In his six years as library director at Columbia, he managed to establish many of the institutions and practices of modern librarianship before he was removed by a Board of Regents fed up with his maverick ways. His longer tenure in New York had more to do with public librarianship and is of less concern here, but it extended his legacy as zealous reformer and bureaucratic brawler going to almost any length to accomplish his goals. Librarians looking for models for competition, innovation, and marketing success need look no further. His rhetoric from a speech in 1888 was remarkably similar to what is heard today: "The old library was passive, asleep . . . , getting in but not giving out . . . ; the librarian a . . . jailer to guard against the escape of the unfortunate under his care. The new library is active, an aggressive, educating force in the community, a living fountain of good influences; . . . and the librarian occupies a field of active usefulness second to none" (Wiegand 1996, 130).

Not all of Dewey's ideas were successful. University of New York Chancellor Whitelaw Reid claimed that "he has as many crank notions as anybody outside of an asylum" (Wiegand 1996, 212). One of them, his dream of a simplified spelling system (for increased literacy), led to ridicule from members of the exclusive club that he founded. In response to such oddities as a menu item listing "Stud Prunes" (stewed prunes) at the club, one William J. Blunt wrote him: "Your rotten way of spelling the English language certainly amuses me. . . . Have a little sense and don't make an ass out of yourself" (Wiegand 1996, 327). All to no avail.

Dewey's radical, far-thinking vision contrasted to the intense discipline and rigid method that he enforced on his subordinates and which he applied to himself in his management style. In meetings with him, staff were required to have their points worked up in advance and expressed in the fewest possible words. Dewey's methods no doubt were influenced by Taylorism, a management practice developed from industrialization that was transforming the nation. The method called for a mechanistic analysis and refinement of processes in terms of time and motion to produce highest efficiency (Budd 2005, 34; Wiegand 1996, 192). To an extent, Dewey was amplifying a powerful cultural current. Taylorism depended on feedback to increase efficiency, and no proponent of assessment today could have surpassed Dewey. His reference service at Columbia featured a box for written comments, but a better sense of his devotion to this principle comes from his personal life.

> At the beginning of each month [Dewey and his wife] would draw up a list of assignments for personal improvement. Annie's categories included: "Exercise 1 hr; Self-Culture, 1 hr; Sing 15 min; Don't waste a minute." Melvil's categories included "Horseback 3 a week; Dress *well*; Short, organized letters; Rise early, eat slowly; Make no promises; Breathe

> deeply, sing, and settle cash daily." At the end of the month
> they rated their performance in each of these categories, and
> discussed progress. (Wiegand 1996, 75)

No staff member who chafed under Dewey's obsessive standards could claim that he did not apply them to himself.

Dewey himself and the rapid growth and subdivision of libraries produced a type of organization that Max Weber first called a bureaucracy in the 1930s (Budd 2005, 134). This was an organization characterized primarily by a subdivision of labor and specialization, operated according to explicit and detailed rules, and arranged into an impersonal hierarchy. Marian the Librarian, as featured in *The Music Man* and *It's a Wonderful Life* (in essentially the same form), dramatized librarians to the outside world as conformist, dull, frustrated, and repressed individuals at the heart of a vast bureaucracy. (Meditating on attitudes toward librarians, Atlas observes: "At least we have been finally deemed relevant enough to have our own 'action' figure" [Atlas, Wallace, and Fleet 2005, 316].) This model persisted through the postwar period, only to be upended by the social turmoil of the 1960s, which had a somewhat different impact on library organization than Taylorism and the move toward rigid hierarchies had in earlier times. Librarians now clamored for equal status with faculty in universities. Nondegreed staff agitated for greater recognition for their work. Both elements crossed the vertical arrangement of a hierarchy with the horizontal one of unionization.

At the start of the twenty-first century, budget crisis, structural change, and technological advances have created a veritable stew of cultures among librarians. The bureaucratic legacy persists—in silos divided along departmental or divisional lines such that one does not know what the other one is doing. The issues of stratification, which unions were designed to address, have not been fully resolved. Age is now an important issue, as part of the profession approaches retirement. There is a significant difference in the culture of older staff, trained to bureaucratic values, and a younger generation of digital natives with different work practices and skills (Zabel 2007, 109). Technology complicates the generational divide, and this is manifested by a common friction between systems departments and the rest of the library (Budd 2005, 56; Davis-Millis and Owens 1997, 102–103; Dougherty and McClure 1997, 71). Given different bodies of knowledge, work practices, technology, and even languages, difficulties are bound to occur. Libraries must organize themselves before they can engage with outside competition.

How to describe the cultures of academic libraries as a first step toward understanding and improving them? To do this, librarians have appealed to the field of organizational development and its various structural models (French and Bell 1999, xii; Grimes 1998, 24, 27). (Our discussion will be confined to those aspects of internal library culture that are most relevant to the design and delivery of library services. We will not be considering other notable aspects of library culture, such as its dedicated opposition to censorship and its representations of itself and its representation by others—all worthy topics in their own right and all deserving of separate treatment.) These structural models correspond with the large-scale evolution of business organizations that has been followed by libraries.

Weber's bureaucracy makes for one model of rigid hierarchy of status, behavior, and communication patterns (Budd 2005, 3, 8, 9, 24; French and Bell 1999, 69; Grimes 1998, 29). Even the internal memo by which bureaucracy functions is said to enforce an authoritarian relationship that closes off discussion by its form alone.

> Memos, frequently in the form of directives, are issued from one of the upper tiers of the hierarchy and disseminated to lower tiers. Many memoranda are written so that no response is necessary; that is, the memo is intended as one-way communication. At times, the questions that might be raised by memos go unasked, because the unidirectional nature of the information suggests that questioning should not be necessary and probably will not be welcomed. Even when these assumptions are incorrect from the viewpoint of the writer of the memo, the nature of the form of communication, combined with the structure of the bureaucracy, sends messages to the recipient of the memo. Those messages may indicate that the memo is not the initiation of a dialogue. (Budd 2005, 137)

Dewey's own dedication to these principles is evident in his use of "P-slips" (the blank side of discarded catalog cards) to communicate. Staff were required to check their pigeonholes several times a day, right next to the desk of Dewey, who typically did not raise his head to look at them. Small wonder that the fundamental rules of such a culture have been described as follows:

1. Bypass embarrassment and threat wherever possible.
2. Act as though you are not bypassing them.
3. Don't discuss steps 1 and 2 while they are happening.
4. Don't discuss the undiscussability of the undiscussable.
   (French and Bell 1999, 54)

This does not encourage a staff to innovate.

A second model backs off from such a monolithic, unitary structure. It considers structure instead from a political point of view as a set of coalitions jockeying for advantage and frequently changing alliances. Not that this was irrelevant to Dewey's method of operation, as he typically joined organizations together (often created for the purpose) and used them strategically. Generally, this second model is applied to environments that are less rigidly structured than the pure bureaucracy. University environments based on semiautonomous academic departments and other units are more relevant to this model than are business corporations (Budd 2005, 31). Various factions typically have to combine in the university environment to accomplish anything; negotiation, maneuvering, and discussion are the modes of operation.

A third model is yet more fluid. Recognizing innumerable factors that influence personnel, including values, circumstances, and opinions as well as overt regulation, this model backs away further from the cause and effect and repeatability that characterize the other models. Such is the complexity at work that the whole is described in terms of an organism each of whose parts interacts with every other part such that no part can be analyzed in isolation; one can understand only the aggregate behavior (Budd 2005, 37; Crawford and Gorman 1995, 180).

While these three models correspond to an evolutionary time course, each model can be applied in principle to any one institution at a given time. This study and the individual cases which follow privilege the third, organic model, yet all three remain relevant today.

Borrowing heavily from the third model, libraries have offered proposals to meet their current challenges, including one that involves becoming "zooming organizations" (Stoffle et al. 2003, 357, 370). This refers to organizations that respond to their environment with continual small changes. There is a widespread rhetoric about the need for "agility" and "nimbleness." The literature on this is extensive (Overall 2009, 191; Ralph and Ellis 2009, 23). To provide a fresh perspective, this study will advance another paradigm which, though related to the others, is largely unfamiliar to libraries. The model comes from military history and theory. Typically, this realm has little to do with libraries, other than through the Patriot Act (although the origins of the Internet within the U.S. Department of Defense suggest that this link may be more fruitful than appears at first glance). The ideas in question were developed by a little-known Air Force pilot, Colonel John Boyd, who cut an unlikely figure as an intellectual (Coram 2002). He began his career in the 1950s as "40-second Boyd," the self-described "greatest fighter pilot in the world." His nickname came from his standing challenge for any pilot to begin a duel placed directly behind his aircraft in a position of greatest advantage where the opponent would be able fire his guns at Boyd without any threat of return fire. Boyd promised to reverse the positions of the aircraft within forty seconds in spite of the best efforts of his opponents. History records that he never failed except for one draw. Boyd acted his part with a loud, profane, aggressive persona, but he had a systematic bent that was less obvious. He sought to develop the principles of air combat into a comprehensive theory that could be used for training. This work first produced a classification of various maneuvers. These were then distilled into a principle, the energy-maneuverability theory, that remains preeminent in aerial combat. The theory was also applied to the development of aircraft design. The key principle turned out to be not any one of the attributes associated with combat planes, such as speed, armament, turn rate, climb rate, range, and so on, but an ability to switch rapidly between them through design features called "fast transients." The hydraulic system for the F-86 Sabre jet flown in Korea, which increased the responsiveness of control surfaces, is one example. This work resulted in a generation of combat planes that ensured American military supremacy through the Cold War and beyond.

Boyd dreamed of more. He wished to transcend air warfare and develop a universal theory for conflict in every form. At this stage, he had grown into a semilegendary figure in the halls of the Pentagon. Walking about in tattered slippers with an abstracted air, he was capable of collaring four-star generals and stabbing his finger into their chests while shouting tirades and showering them with spittle. His own group of devoted acolytes believed that he no longer "had both oars in the water." Nonetheless, Boyd produced his theory. Drawing together military theory (with an emphasis on the Chinese sage Sun Tzu) as well as quantum physics and thermodynamics, he proposed that change was a fundamental attribute of the universe and that any entity needed to change with it to survive. In a presentation that ballooned into thirteen hours of slides and monologue, Boyd argued that the critical attribute of the successful competitor in *any* environment was the abstract one of *speed of decision cycling* (see Coram 2002, 335, 338; see also Newman 2010). This was elaborated into a model called the OODA loop (for *observe, orient, decide,* and *act*). Observation entails gathering data; orientation, the formulation of choices; decision, the selection among choices; and action, carrying out the choice. This sequence of activities, reiterated faster than by any competitor, defined a winning strategy. It applied equally to airplanes, battlefield tactics, the business world, and literally anything that could be framed as a competition. The United States Marine Corps actively embraced this theory in its tactical doctrine, and there are hints that Boyd himself was the architect of the radical strategy of maneuver that underpinned the First Gulf War.

Boyd's ultimate obscurity cannot be chalked up to the dictates of operational secrecy alone. Boyd's radical new ideas and uncompromising pursuit of them, as with Dewey, earned him enemies. He became a pariah in the military and was never permitted by the Air Force to fly the F-16 fighter plane that he helped to design. Yet the military was all too happy to adopt his ideas, which have also been embraced by the corporate and sports worlds, proliferating far beyond what Boyd himself could have imagined. They've even been applied recently by libraries, in ILL and other service areas (Bridges 2004). Any reference to "decision cycling" in the discourse of policy originates with Boyd. There is something fitting about librarians reaching out to another visionary nonconformist like Dewey for new ideas in a time of change and redefinition.

Boyd's ideas also appeal to this study because of their high stakes. Libraries now talk in terms of their very survival, and there is no reason not to draw upon theories designed for this purpose. Second, the radical generality of Boyd's theories promises that there should be some application. Thus, the instrumentality of fast transients and speed of decision cycling will be one set of criteria to judge how our case studies are negotiating the seven categories of issues that we have discussed up to this point.

Part Two :: Case Studies

::

University of California, Davis

The University of California, Davis, is one of ten campuses that together constitute one of the largest public university systems in the United States. UCD's own roots reach back to the beginning of the settlement of the California territory by American pioneers in the nineteenth century. The edge of the Sacramento Valley proved to be a fertile agricultural area; it became a crossroads, center of commerce, and ultimately the town of Davis, named for Jerome C. Davis, who assembled a 12,000-acre property on the current site of the university. (See Scheuring 2001; this is the definitive history of the University of California, Davis.) However, when the University of California was formed in 1868 as an outgrowth of the Morrill Act of 1862, which established land grant universities, the agricultural department was located with the main campus at Berkeley. The affiliation of Davis with the University of California began with the establishment of the University Farm there in 1906. This organization served as a laboratory for agricultural experiments for the university as well as a site for vocational training for farmers. The University Farm was the agricultural core of the land grant mission at the University of California.

Known for a cheerful, placid sense of community derived from its farming culture, the school at Davis continued to grow in size. Teacher training was added to agricultural training in the curriculum, and the school admitted women in numbers after World War I. As the quality and scope of the education improved, a movement sought to raise Davis from its status as a satellite of Berkeley to an independent campus. The library, which had been informally kept within a series of buildings, gained its first dedicated facility as part of an administration building constructed on the south side of the campus quad in the mid-1940s. Created entirely by administrators without any consultation with librarians, the building was heavily compromised from the start. The size of its collection was limited because of its dual purpose, and the building lacked cooling devices to off-set the 110-degree heat of summers in the Sacramento Valley.

Nevertheless, the library and the school persevered, and the campus achieved independent status in 1959. This event coincided with the publication of the California Master Plan for Higher Education (1960), which outlined the creation of a system of large public universities that would drive the economic, educational, and social progress of the state. The subsequent christening of California as the Golden State and its status as the American ideal validated this investment into higher education. The challenge of the new campus at Davis was to offer a complete modern university education while remaining true to the original agricultural purpose of the campus as well as its intangible communal culture, known as the "Davis advantage." A particular milestone to this end was the establishment of the School of Veterinary Medicine in 1948. With its historical base in agriculture and its extensive facilities and stocks of animals, the veterinary school possessed intrinsic advantages, and combining these with a forward-looking practical curriculum, the school rose rapidly to the top of its field, ranking first in the nation in 1980 and remaining at or near the top ever since. The library grew along with the campus and the profession as a whole in the latter twentieth century. At its height, as many as five branches operated: the main library at the original quad location, named after Judge Peter J. Shields; the Physical Sciences and Engineering Library on the south side of campus; the Carlson Health Sciences Library next to the veterinary school on the west side of campus; an agricultural/economics department library housed and funded by its sponsoring departments on the quad; and the Blaisdell Medical Library at the UC Davis Medical Center in Sacramento. The collection has particular strengths in agriculture and animal science and boasts comprehensive collections in the areas of viticulture, enology, nematology, bee biology, and historical agricultural technology.

At the outset of the twenty-first century, UC Davis looks very different than its origins as a university farm might suggest, yet its roots remain. The original agricultural purpose has grown and transformed into a focus on sustainability and environmental issues, which are being pursued from all the different viewpoints of its many, thriving departments. A new institution, West Village, seeks to integrate academic study and residential life practices together into an ongoing experiment in sustainability. This sensitivity to the environment and spirit of tolerance circulates throughout the rest of campus in a vast throng of cyclists, which has led the city to proclaim itself as the biking capital of the United States. Faculty, students, and staff pedal among a network of paths and among the entirely student-operated buses—turning, merging, and sometimes colliding, but bringing it all off in a spirit of calm cooperation.

Meanwhile, owing to a confluence of circumstances, the recent history of the UCD Library is one of a tumult that would have challenged Melvil Dewey himself. As with the rest of the profession, the economic crash of 2008 brought into sharp focus the steady decline in funding and resources that had afflicted the UCD Library for over a decade. Even amidst national disaster, California's plight loomed large. In 2009, the UC system faced over $637 million in funding cuts along with significant other reductions (University of California, Commission on the Future 2010, 132). The UCD Library found itself with a debt of approximately $1 million.

The statistical snapshot of the UCD Library shown in table 1 is consistent with the general profile of academic libraries. Collection growth is slowing. Service activity, staff numbers, and the budget are in slow decline. The library administration responded to the 2008 budget cuts with a global reconsideration of all categories of operations: services, collection, and staff; meanwhile, the staff was solicited for "big ideas." Two proposals, having to do with the closing of an offsite storage area and the return of some vacant positions to the university, proved useful, and the library was able to pay off its debt even in the worst of times.

Yet events did not stand still. California's Proposition 30 in the 2012 election loomed as the next challenge. This proposal by Governor Jerry Brown aimed to stabilize California's tattered finances with radical (for California) tax increases, much of which went toward funding in education. Upon this depended the future health of UC. "All of the belt-tightening has already happened. If Prop 30 does not get passed, they are thinking in terms of shutting down whole departments," predicted MacKenzie Smith, University Librarian at UCD (Smith 2013). Just as the nation agonized over the hotly contested presidential election, the library agonized with the rest of California over Prop 30. The measure passed with 53.9 percent of the vote. Having become quite recently an example of what not to do, California is just now being hailed as a financial model for the rest of the nation (Bradley 2012). It has, at least, enabled UCD to maintain a flat budget, which Smith considers a success.

Reference

This tumultuous climate has reshaped the reference service—the outward face of the library—within the past few years. At its height, and until very recently, the Shields Library offered a highly articulated triage

Table 1. Vital Statistics, UC Davis Library, 2009–2010

Collection	4,175,047
(0% to 13% change in last 5 years)	
Circulation	516,426
(–2% to 13% change in last 5 years)	
ILL:	
Lending	15,335
(–12% to 30% change in last 5 years)	
Borrowing	15,378
(–22% to 14% change in last 3 years)	
Shelf space occupied	75%
Reference transactions	60,592
(–32% to 41% change in last 5 years)	
Instruction to groups	1,004
(15% to 41% change in last 5 years)	
Staff	200
(–16% to 9% change in last 5 years)	
Budget	$19,867,098
(–10% to 2% change in last 5 years)	

Source: Official ARL Statistics (Kyrillidou and Bland 2008, 2009; Kyrillidou and Morris 2011; Kyrillidou, Morris, and Roebuck 2011; Kyrillidou and Young 2008).

Note: Parentheses indicate the highest and lowest rates of annual change in the preceding five years, not necessarily in order.

service with specialized desks for its divisional structure. Patrons entering on the ground floor were greeted by an information desk staffed by librarians and paraprofessionals who answered simple directional questions or routed patrons to subject specialists. Government documents librarians staffed a desk near their collection on the lower level. Humanities and social sciences staffed a desk on the second floor, and the biology/agriculture department staffed a desk on the third floor. In 2009, the government documents department was dissolved as an administrative entity. The physical collection was retained, while the subject specialists were distributed among the humanities/social sciences and biology/agriculture departments. This followed a national trend in which government documents departments have been reduced because of the shift of government information to an online format (eliminating the need for a physical facility) and to compensate for hiring freezes in other departments.

This development paved the way for a more radical change in 2010. All reference desks were closed, and staff (and students) were rotated into a single reference desk on the first floor in a large reception area just to the left of the main entrance. While (as some staff noted) there was no monetary saving, this centralization aimed to streamline the organization and enable a smoother transition toward a smaller staff and reduced resources in the future. To manage the overflow of questions (in terms of both quantity and difficulty), patrons were referred to subject specialists who experimented with various forms of office hours. The library also made the leap into chat reference.

In 2010, the four members of the instruction department began staffing QuestionPoint, a chat service operated by OCLC that had been adopted by other UC campuses. The staff worked two one-hour shifts per week separate from desk reference. Thanks to chat, a twenty-four-hour virtual reference desk was now available to UCD students to make up for the reduced physical reference desks (although this came at a price of being required to devote library staff to other universities, in some cases outside of the UC system altogether). Initially, both the library staff and certain patrons expressed frustration when the chat librarian was not at the campus of inquiry and, in some cases, could not help. Yet the number of users has risen steadily (see fig. 2), a pattern that closely reflects usage for the UC system as a whole (fig. 3).

Ken Furuta, a librarian at UC Riverside who maintains statistics for QuestionPoint use throughout the system, speculates on the inflection points when usage increased for UC: "Our numbers exploded beginning around April 2008 when Qwidget was introduced. There is another increase in January/February 2009 when we joined 24/7. After that, the trends are about the same" (Furuta 2012). The marketing of reference here obviously played a key role.

Assessment of the physical reference service has proven more difficult. Undoubtedly, service has diminished compared to the full triage model. Yet numbers cannot measure exactly how service has changed with the different configuration of the reference desks. Changes in physical location have been matched by changes in responsibility and procedure for keeping statistics, and the data in the resulting records are difficult to interpret. There is an even more fundamental issue with reference statistics. Amy Kautzman, Associate University Librarian at UCD, observes that after a general announcement to the staff that ARL data showed a 40 percent decline in reference use for the campus, the statistics showed a sudden surge in activity! Indeed, given the various definitions of reference categories and the variety of interactions with patrons, either of which can interfere with recording, small wonder that there is a degree of uncertainty in the statistics. The very act of recording them is an assessment, but who assesses the assessors to make sure their recording is accurate? It

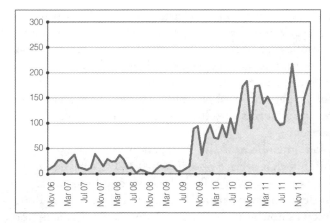

Fig. 2. QuestionPoint chat sessions by quarter, UC Davis Library, November 2006 to November 2011.

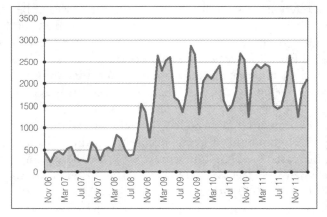

Fig. 3. QuestionPoint chat sessions by quarter, UC library system, November 2006 to November 2011.

would seem that the superstructure of reference statistics driving the various theories and trends in the literature rests on a shaky foundation in the accuracy of the statistics themselves. One plan to address this problem would include student focus groups. Meanwhile, Chancellor Linda Katehi of UCD has asked all units of the campus to undertake detailed assessment plans to be used as a basis for campus planning and the distribution of funds. However, Kautzman notes that while the library and other units can generate data on their own, the value of such data will be limited until a coordinated campus effort comes into place that allows the library to assess the population that it serves and correlate its activities with those of other units. Scott Bennett, University Librarian Emeritus at Yale and a library building consultant, makes a similar point about the inverse relationship between the campus and its library. "Global outcomes get pretty dilute when you get to a school or department, so it's hard to register their impact" (Bennett 2012).

In 2011, the Shields Library reopened reference desks for humanities/social sciences and biology/agriculture during afternoon weekday hours. This is intended as a transition stage toward a fully developed Learning Commons on the first floor of the library together with a café. As the policy remains in flux, a discussion has arisen on the basic values of reference and the best way to realize them. Marcia Meister, a government documents specialist with thirty years of experience, favors subject specialist desks. A multipurpose, centrally located desk of the kind that has been tried suffers from poor acoustics, active traffic around the desk, and the lack of access to a reference collection, she says (Meister 2012). David Michalski, a subject specialist in the humanities and social sciences and reference librarian, shares these concerns as well as philosophical attitudes toward reference.

Reference at its best, he argues, has a critical teaching function. Using the full scope of the reference interview, librarians must elicit in person the goal of each patron, who may not have formulated it themselves. As part of formulating a question and exploring the literature, the librarian can "impart search techniques, and convey the peculiarities of a discourse's publication and distribution. . . . The librarian can work to put the researcher's project in context with the wider intellectual environment. The new perspective built through conversations can lead to new paths of discovery" (Michalski 2011a, 2). These higher level critical functions, normally associated with graduate study and professional scholarship, are also the province of the reference librarian. While the current environment of change imposes restrictions on library service, Michalski argues that the need for high-level reference and critical thinking skills becomes more and not less urgent (Michalski 2011a, 4). The explosion of information, together with the interdisciplinary character of research, makes it more imperative that researchers have an awareness of their discursive environment and other critical skills. The inevitable question is how to transmit education at this level to the patron. Clearly, the old triage system offered clear advantages for consultation. On the other hand, the budgetary demands of the current times aren't going away. Michalski suggests that what is important is a commitment to advanced education to be pursued in any environment.

Heart of Campus

The reference service at Shields is intertwined with the architecture of the building. Yet senior librarians object to the reference desk itself, with its large surrounding space and its high volume of moving traffic. Bennett,

Fig. 4. West (main)
entrance to the Peter J.
Shields Library.

generalizing about the institution of the reference desk, concurs: "You
have a highly paid staff member to direct traffic, to do transactions and
referrals. What a silly waste. . . . I hate reference desks as you can tell. . . .
You're not getting the relationship at that desk that the highly paid staff
member is trained to do" (Bennett 2012). The role of the desk served as
the basis for an entire architecture course developed cooperatively by the
library's art and architecture specialist, Dan Goldstein, and Assistant Professor of Architecture Mark Kessler. Students were asked to redesign the
reference area for greater functionality.

Kessler explains how in the entrance to the library, "traditional and
static elements of Beaux-Arts planning float within a modern open floor
plan." Yet this hybridization "plugs up" the floor space with "elements of
limited use to the library." The desk is not ideally situated. The interior,
Kessler continues, seeks "to recall the great public libraries of the City
Beautiful era, many of which proved to be more successful as institutional
symbols than as functioning libraries" (Kessler 2012). The Shields Library, as shown also by its entrance, suffers from monumentalism (fig. 4).

As it turns out, the service problems addressed by the students
opened up architectural issues of much larger scope. The problem is not
the placement of reference in the building, but the entrance itself and ultimately the entire building. Nested originally into an administration
building, the Shields Library has proceeded with ad hoc additions. The
original rectangular building on the south side of the campus quad has
added three similar additions over time to create a four-sided enclosure
around an inner courtyard, with the original building serving as the north
side. The entrance has been shifted among three of the four wings. Originally, the entrance on the north side of the building opened directly onto

the quad. The entrance was then shifted east and then west where it currently is located. The latest iteration has had unexpected, deleterious effects on the entire campus. By supplanting the quad-side entrance, "the west wing of Shields institutionalizes the abandonment of the Quad" (Kessler 2011, 4). Moreover, the plaza leading up to the impressive west entrance bulges into and disrupts a central walk that bordered the west side of the library and formed a straight line from the quad on the north side of the library to Mrak Hall, the central administration building, on the south side. The disruption interferes with a campus atmosphere of communication and leaves Mrak Hall "braced for confrontation" (Kessler 2011, 4). Could the architecture of the library influence campus politics on the outside as well as reference on the inside?

Students proposed various plans for reopening the north entrance to the library on the Quad and thus opening for activity the interior courtyard, which currently maintains an attitude of somnolescence beneath an enormous arching oak tree. Campus planning, meanwhile, is contemplating an even more far-reaching solution. Limited by the town on its east side, campus growth has been forced west and south. To organize development, Bob Segar, UCD's campus planner, has formulated several design strategies. The first is to reanimate the "Civic Core" by consolidating the major cultural elements of campus—the library, the quad, and the administration building—into a single north-south axis (fig. 5). The library stands at the intersection of the north-south and east-west axes. Westward growth is consolidated along an east-west axis built around a bike and bus thoroughfare (fig. 6). Rather than interrupting campus commerce, the library will link it together, serving as a renewed heart of the university.

Go West

Other issues involving physical facilities have had additional effects on library service. The science division of the UCD Library has been dispersed among separate buildings. The biology/agriculture department occupies the third floor of Shields. The Physical Sciences and Engineering Library (PSE) in its own building serves the physical sciences on the south side of campus. The Carlson Health Sciences Library on the far west of campus serves the veterinary school. The agriculture/economics library operates as a departmental library within its sponsoring departments on the quad. And the Blaisdell Medical Library at the Sacramento campus serves the medical school. Over time, the growth of the physical collection caused rearrangements such that subjects were spread among the various buildings in an unintuitive way and pick-up locations for document delivery

and ILL became confusing for patrons. The library budget crisis high-
lighted these problems amid the imperative for greater efficiency. The
agriculture/economics library was closed down. Another idea was to shut
down PSE, saving the operating costs for that building, but this proposal
met with such vigorous resistance from the faculty that a direct appeal
was made to the then new chancellor, Linda Katehi, who postponed the
plan pending further study.

The science departments also proposed to reorganize. The biology/
agriculture departments and health sciences would be consolidated into
one, with staff circulating between two locations, Shields and Carlson, on
opposite sides of the campus. One motive was a reduction in staff positions. But another driver came from campus policy completely outside of
the library. As part of a general renovation of the veterinary school, the
office of the dean of that school proposed to relocate within the Carlson
Library. Carlson thus stood to lose half of its space. But what seemed to
be a setback also offered opportunities that lay nascent in Sacramento
within the Blaisdell Medical Library.

In some ways, the story of the Blaisdell Library prefigures that of
Carlson. In 2006, a new medical education building was created that incorporated the library and physically joined it to the units it served—

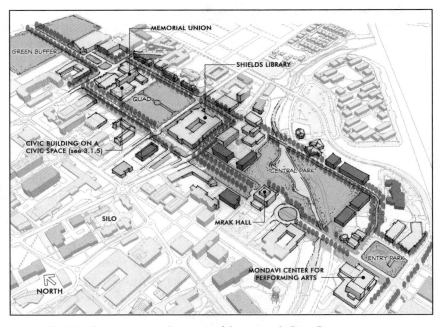

Fig. 5. Shields Library occupies the center of the campus's Civic Core.

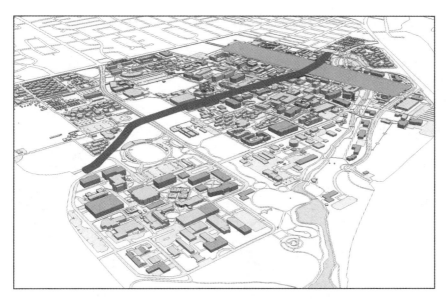

Fig. 6. The Civic Core (*rectangle, top right*) and Bike/Bus Boulevard (*thick line*) organize the campus. Shields Library sits where they intersect.

the medical school, the nursing school, and the Center for Health and Technology. The building consists of two towers connected by passageways at every floor, with the library occupying the ground floor of one tower. The main advantage of the new structure is the library's proximity to the medical school's education facilities. Library staff can walk over to instruction rooms in the opposite tower, and medical school faculty and staff can walk into the library to use the collection or consult with the staff. "It gives us easy access to our major clientele," notes Rebecca Davis, acting department head at the Blaisdell Medical Library. Since the opening of the new facility, reference, instruction, gate count, and collection use statistics have all risen significantly, with the highest increases in instruction (350 percent) and gate count (60 percent).

As part of a commitment to new technology, the library has invested heavily in e-books, but Davis observes that students seem not to be interested in them. "They want to be able to have their laptop open. Maybe they're taking notes. Maybe they will have a book here and a book there. And maybe even a book online. But it's a lot easier to go from book to book when you've got them lying in front of you. That's my experience with it" (Davis 2012). One might wish to see the actual e-book usage statistics for Blaisdell, but actually finding this seemingly straightforward

**Table 2. MD Consult and First Consult sessions per month
at UC libraries, January–October 2012**

	MD Consult[1] licensed sessions	First Consult[1] licensed sessions	First Consult app downloads	First Consult app visits
Jan.	9,983	348	6	12
Feb.	9,382	273	0	10
Mar.	7,967	252	3	35
Apr.	7,482	200	1	0
May	7,614	195	1	0
June	5,906	107	4	0
July	6,918	117	3	13
Aug.	8,212	83	0	12
Sept.	8,209	306	1	1
Oct.	23,300	344	5	3
YTD	94,973	2,225	24	86

Source: MD Consult.
1. First Consult and MD Consult are medical research tools owned by the publisher Elsevier.

and essential information turned out to be surprisingly difficult. Rather than being consolidated in one place, it is kept by each of the vendors supplying e-books, of which there are four: AccessMedicine, STAT!Ref, MD Consult, and Ovid. These must be consulted individually. Requests for MD Consult and STAT!Ref had to be sent through CDL, which handles electronic licenses for the UC system. The MD Consult report is shown in table 2, which shows usage for the UC system as a whole. There is a steady if slight downward trend in the numbers, but it is impossible to infer the usage at Blaisdell.

STAT!Ref did not respond at all to the request for data. Access-Medicine made its data available directly from a website. But the request form raised significant questions about what exactly "usage" might be. Is it the number of sessions opened in the interface? Is it the number of searches run within the interface? Is it the number of times the product is downloaded? There was data for each of these parameters. Figure 7, which shows number of sessions, proves roughly representative. The hills and

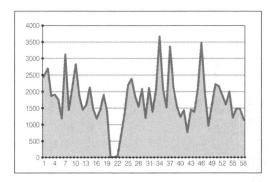

Fig. 7. AccessMedicine sessions per month, UC Davis, January 2008 to October 2012.

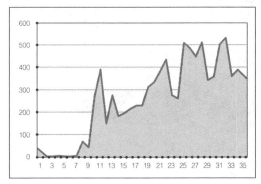

Fig. 8. Ovid e-book titles retrieved per month, UC Davis, 2010–2012.

valleys of usage define a slight but steady downward trajectory. The charts for content downloads and number of searches follow a similar downward trend. Ovid returned data for e-book titles with a significantly different trend (fig. 8). This set of data, however, applies to the entire campus, so it is impossible to tell which books are for medicine. As a whole the numerical data may be consistent with Davis's impression of low use by medical patrons, but the data is really inadequate for testing this claim. The data speaks more to the fog of uncertainty surrounding assessment as described by Kautzman and to issues of content control by vendors.

In any case, the e-books are just part of a determined educational mission at Blaisdell utilizing evidence-based medicine, which is in the process of transforming both medical practice and education. Evidence-based medicine reorganizes medical literature into a model of a pyramid (fig. 9). The base of the pyramid consists of research studies analogous to scholarship in other disciplines. Ascending above them are more specialized types of studies, culminating at the apex with systematic reviews and

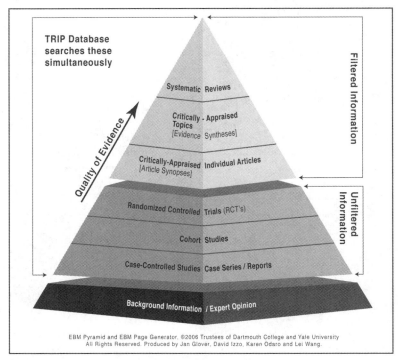

Fig. 9. Evidence-Based Medicine Pyramid.

meta-analyses that distill the literature into specific recommendations for practicing physicians (Abbott 2012). The top level may constitute a new (quaternary?) member of the traditional classification of research literature into primary, secondary, and tertiary. Evidence-based studies accomplish the reflective, analytical work that has been the province of researchers themselves. It has changed medical practice by making the literature more accessible to practicing physicians and presumably increasing the effectiveness of health care.

In medical education, evidence-based medicine is making inroads into the much-maligned lecture method where students are exposed to far more information than they can hope to retain. While the traditional system ultimately produces highly trained doctors, it is enormously inefficient and wasteful. Evidence-based medicine utilizes a new problem-solving approach whereby entering students, working in teams, can apply concepts to problems, thus motivating themselves to learn the material and practicing analytic and communication skills in the process. A knowledge of research tools and methods is important for this type of education, and the Blaisdell Library is central to this effort. Nonetheless, its initiatives have endured a fiery trial. Davis observes that, at first, the goal-oriented medical personnel with their demanding schedules were highly resistant to instruction in databases. But once they were introduced, "We got rave reviews." To further assist research, the Blaisdell Library operates a novel document delivery service. For material which is not available electronically to medical patrons, the library will scan print materials in the Blaisdell Library or from any of the holdings of the main campus or its offsite-storage facility and deliver them to the patron.

This integrated model of education with its document delivery service appeared to offer new possibilities for the Carlson Library to serve the veterinary school and the entire campus. The scale of possibility initiated a dialogue on the values of librarianship among the staff. Some questions were raised by Axel Borg, senior librarian for the biology/agriculture department and head of the library's world-famous collections in viticulture and enology. He points out that medical researchers do not necessarily share the same culture as other scientists, and that it may be a risky assumption that what appeals to one group appeals to the other. "Disciplines in the transition from paper to electronic are moving at different rates and move at different distances down this continuum . . . and that has to be accounted for in the near term," Borg observes. He continues, "The users of the paper collection come over here because they know what they're looking for, they know how it's structured." Life sciences faculty, for example, may have a different relationship to their physical collections. Ultimately, buy-in from the stakeholders is both crucial and unpredictable, as it proved to be with the abortive plan to close PSE. Like Michalski, Borg argues for serious liaison work, walking collections, and the building of personal relationships. "When I started in this profession almost 30 years ago, it was 'Well, everything's going to be on the computer . . .' Well, all of my professional life has been this transition, and I think it's going to continue to take some time to do it." But with a senior project manager already assigned to the renovation of Carlson by campus planning, funds were cut, and the vision went glimmering.

Leadership

In addition to dealing with its physical facilities and budget issues, UCD, in this same period, grappled with its leadership structure after the sudden retirement after twenty-five years of Marilyn Sharrow, University

Librarian. Her position was filled in 2012 with MacKenzie Smith, who worked at Harvard University and MIT, where she played a leading role in adapting their libraries, research, and teaching programs to the "emerging technological landscape" (Smith 2013; see also University of California, Davis 2012). As Research Director at MIT, she served as project manager of the DSpace open-source software platform for digital archives, which has become the dominant technology for university repositories. Its rise among a field of heavy competition is a "long story," she notes. But much of its success lay with a determination to make it portable. "It's a turnkey system—an institutional repository in a box. You don't have to build entire applications to make it work," she says. But by the same token, it is easy to modify. "Some of the commercial competitors to DSpace, and there are many, have fallen by the wayside or failed because you can't change them. Nobody gets these things right the first time, so you need something that you can adapt" (Smith 2013). Boyd's principle of adaptability manifests itself here in the details of software design.

Upon arrival, Smith was immediately tasked with developing a strategic plan as part of Chancellor Katehi's comprehensive plan to push UCD to become one of the top-five research universities in the nation. Smith, who has conducted strategic planning efforts and reorganizations at Harvard and MIT and as a consultant to other libraries, notes that a process that ordinarily takes over a year was completed in six months with the library's first strategic plan for 2013–2016. A town hall meeting introduced the process in September 2012. In October and November, library staff could sign up for two half-day workshops with exercises for thinking about the strategic plan and providing feedback. The material was processed by Smith and her department heads and the plan draft unveiled in another town hall in January 2013. The keys to successful planning, according to Smith, are "pretty well understood at this point. It has to be broadly consultative but it has to have strong leadership." Surveys were conducted of undergraduate and graduate students (with faculty to come), advisory groups were formed, and administrators consulted. "The process was compressed but not truncated" (Smith 2013). Given the usual time frame of a year, Smith says that she would have brought in outside experts to educate the library staff on the issues involved.

The budget remains the fundamental reality behind the library's future. Although the library succeeded in attaining a flat budget, this coincided with a commitment by the university not to raise tuition for a number of years; it also coincided with a decrease in the state's already small commitment to the university's budget of about 8 percent. With these restrictions, the only way for the university to sustain itself is to increase the number of students, according to Smith. Planning must also account for the related phenomenon that too many students are not graduating on time.

The draft strategic plan (which continues to undergo review and consultation) can be distilled graphically as shown in figure 10. Fundamental to this design, according to Smith, was coherence, with linkages clearly established from the university's strategic plan down to areas of focus for the library. This provides a framework for accountability and assessment. The library's streamlined mission and vision statements at the bottom and the more granular "facets" at the top serve to bracket and bathe the library plan that is schematized between them. In a broad image of the tension between "high tech" and "high touch," the left side is devoted to infrastructure improvements and the right to programmatic changes, although each side repeats within itself the dynamics of both.

Some examples will have to suffice as we review the plan. Element #1, "Online Platform," has to do with new tools for, among other things, the support of scholarly communication. The demands here are driven by UCD's dual niche as an autonomous entity and as part of the larger UC system. CDL has created for UC a scholarly repository and a number of related tools of broad influence in the profession (to be discussed more fully in the next chapter). But powerful and innovative as they are, they do not, with the current state of technology, quite meet the needs of the nonexpert end-user, according to Smith. "There's tons of open-source tools out there, but what I'm talking about are tools that will help the library take advantage of the infrastructure that's out there, whether it's CDL's or Amazon's or somebody else's. There's something in between, and that's where the library would help" (Smith 2013).

Such a goal builds upon work that has been under way at UCD for more than a decade. Since 2002 Jared Campbell, metadata librarian at UCD, has worked with four separate projects, helping to organize and mount their data. These include creating a union catalog of anthropological archives and a digital archive of United Farm Workers contracts and devising how to organize and make available collections from the Bohart Museum of Entomology. Each project was highly labor-intensive and required the adaptation of a unique set of tools, including MetaGrove, Almagest, Koha, and MarcEdit, and the creation of new tools such as tables for relational databases and new metadata schemes. The projects have not been without their problems, which have included "limitations of the open-source tools, problems securing ongoing financial resources and personnel, and failures in coming to agreement on project specifications" (Campbell 2012). As part of its strategic plan, UCD is looking to introduce standardization and simplicity with a user orientation along the lines of DSpace.

The imperative for the programmatic side of the plan is to scale up services to meet the new, enlarged student body. Element #3, "Education," in part looks to transform instruction from traditional modes to remote technology. "MOOCs [massive online open courses] have revolutionized the whole way that people think about online education," according to Smith. They happen to be an ideal tool for UCD to accommodate an enlarged student population. "We have to go online because there's no way you can scale the in-classroom approach that we do now," adds Smith. Upscaling also applies to element #4, "Collections," a traditional stronghold of UCD. These collections will be maintained, but not with the goal of building the largest collection for its own sake. Stewardship, the core concept of the mission statement, means, according to Smith, not only holding on to your materials but also disseminating them. This includes digitizing for outside access, connecting to other collections of value, and making sure that the collection remains harmonized to the university's goals as they evolve.

Transcendence

Implicit in the strategic plan is the fact that in addition to its own rich history, UCD has a second identity as part of a system. With its tightly integrated campuses, UC is perhaps more aware than most such systems of the imperative for shared collections, and the need to transcend duplicate collections in favor of a shared repository. "It does not make sense in anybody's world that we're paying the hundreds of thousands of dollars that we pay on every campus to have these separate catalogs. It's insane," said Kautzman. UC has sought to address the need for more collaboration with an ambitious project that combines a comprehensive review of technical services systemwide with new technology in the form of a redesigned interface for the system catalog called Melvyl. (The rationale for the project is described in detail in its original document [Bibliographic Services Task Force 2005].) There are many issues in play, including the need to merge the outmoded and often incompatible online public access catalogs (OPACs) of member libraries, eliminate duplication of cataloging efforts between campuses, coordinate and automate ILL processing and ordering, modify workflows in the technical services of campuses to take advantage of systemwide

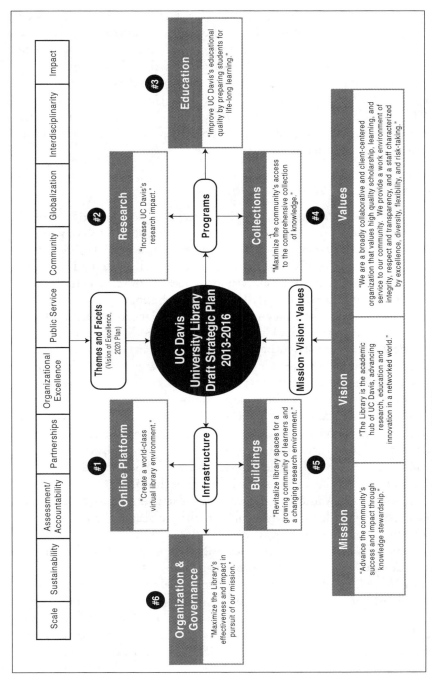

Fig. 10. University Library Strategic Plan, 2013–2016, UC Davis.

improvements, and design an improved interface for the systemwide catalog. These issues, in turn, have a host of ramifications, such as the need to coordinate acquisitions among the campuses and to negotiate licenses, with all the issues of administration that flow from that. In fact, this global project is a laboratory for understanding all of the issues related to building, administering, and delivering a shared collection. UCD, as a node within this system, provides a vantage point for viewing the project in action, and this will be done, first, through an examination of the interface to Melvyl.

Quest for the "White Whale"

The new interface design of Melvyl is a technological initiative derived from the argument that if libraries are being outcompeted by commercial search engines and Amazon, why not imitate their success? The model for this naturally is Google, whose many innovations have swept all before it. Thrown into relief by the new vision of radical simplicity, traditional OPACs cry out for streamlining. This includes eliminating command-line interfaces and extensive limit choices. The MARC record, a technical tool necessary for librarians but of little use to most patrons, has been removed from view. Likewise, barriers between formats have been reduced. Patrons often have difficulty understanding that books and periodicals require different search tools, so article results now mingle with books. The holdings of different campuses have been combined together with a screen that shows which campuses hold a particular item, and forms have been put in place to submit ILL requests. In a spirit of broad access, the materials of the HathiTrust, a digital repository, have been indexed in Melvyl. In the latest version of Melvyl, the WorldCat Local service developed by OCLC allows patrons to access the contents of the WorldCat database in a more user-friendly interface than the older FirstSearch one. Patrons can now choose, via a drop-down menu, whether to search their campus library, the UC system, or WorldCat.

Based on this foundation of accessibility, a host of plans are in place for additional Web 2.0–style improvements. To complete a modern look, records for Melvyl display images of book covers like those at Amazon. The left sidebar is filled with options to refine a search by various limits, including format and database. Recommendations for further searches are also posted on the left sidebar and classified among parameters such as author, year, language, topic, and more. (See fig. 11.) In another clear nod to Web 2.0, users can post review comments. The rationale for the front

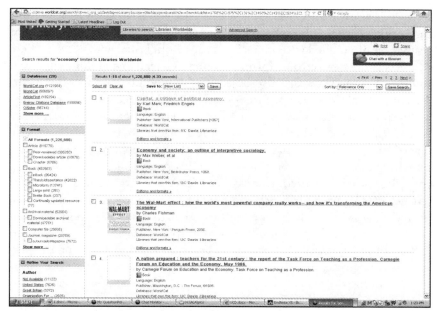

Fig. 11. The display of search results in Melvyl.

end has been thought out in depth in terms of technological trends.

Naturally, assessment is crucial to such a far-flung and ambitious project, and the project task force, in cooperation with OCLC, has been diligent in gathering feedback. Multiple usability studies have been run at UC campuses (supplemented by OCLC's research among other users of its products). Users from a range of service categories, including students and faculty, have been interviewed at length regarding their experience with Melvyl. The subjects have undergone performance tests, and eye-tracking studies are planned for the future to analyze responses to every detail of the interface. Overall, the results have been extremely positive, with each of the major innovations garnering approval. The advisory group for the production phase of Melvyl, the Melvyl Advisory Group (MAG), continues to process feedback, which is reported to systemwide user groups, library staff, and WorldCat and addresses those issues that "bubble to the top," according to Patricia Martin, director of the Discovery & Delivery services at CDL, one of the original developers of Melvyl, and convener for MAG.

However, in the midst of these favorable results, a dissenting voice appears to be struggling to make itself heard. Some frontline librarians have objected to the new interface. They point to a reduced search capability. For known titles, Melvyl is not as efficient as local OPACs in finding results. Others object to inconsistencies among the results. Lists of results are often filled with items from the HathiTrust, which, even where listed as being in electronic form, are often not available in full-text, creating frustration. There are also objections among librarians to the inclusion of journal titles, which, rather than increasing access, are seen as cluttering and confusing results. Adam Siegel, Slavic languages bibliographer at UCD, observed, "They're adding some article tools, but not all of them. There's the implication that you can scan all the scholarly literature that's out there. Look no further. But that's only a subset and a small subset at that. It's heavily slanted towards Anglo-American science literature" (Siegel 2012). Michalski argues that apart from particular functions, Melvyl affects search behavior in a way that undermines good research methods that librarians should be trying to inculcate. "Research, which has traditionally relied on a process of critical reflection, based on the play of both similarities and differences, [is] being transformed into the problem of finding the expected and the similar. . . . Instead of an invitation to exploration and trailblazing we have a slot to insert one figure in order to return its like-value" (Michalski 2011b, 4).

The panorama of response displays anomalies. High-level system administration and end-users, seemingly at the opposite ends of the organizational spectrum, appear to be harmonized. They are supported by usability studies carried out with systematic methodology. On the other hand, some front-line librarians, who form the link between the two ends of the spectrum, have expressed notably different opinions. As a further complicating factor, the source of librarian criticism remains elusive. The formal mechanisms of feedback have not captured significant criticism, but it persists in informal venues such as testy exchanges at systemwide meetings, on library blogs, and in surveys on other topics. Perhaps the difficulty lies in the perceived purpose of Melvyl and the priorities behind its technology. Kautzman, a member of the original task force which developed Melvyl, observes, "We really wanted user satisfaction to be our number one principle . . . and for most undergraduate papers, it rocks. But if you are someone who's worked in a very specialized database, if you work with MEDLINE and you're working with doctors and so on then it will be less satisfactory." As MAG seeks to align its project goals, its user satisfaction, and its gatekeeping frontline librarians into a harmonious whole, Melvyl illustrates the challenges of building a centralized catalog. "We were able to do a lot of things that we wanted to, but there's a lot more to do," Kautzman concludes.

Enterprise

Melvyl's Next Generation Technical Services (NGTS) deals with the back end of library services in the form of technical processing. One major goal is to improve the efficiency of workflows by removing duplication and making appropriate use of new technology. With a project of this magnitude, the first order of the day was to figure out how to proceed and determine the administrative structures that would be necessary. Given the choices of going top-down or bottom-up, the policy that emerged was to do both. Teams were organized to do environmental scans to identify problems and set priorities. Meanwhile, the individual campuses were enjoined to undertake "enterprise-level" initiatives (Council of University Librarians 2010). More recently, the NGTS management team, taking a cue from Boyd and his "fast transients," has created a structure designed for speed. Selected individuals from throughout the system are organized into teams of three (knows as Power of Three groups), each with a domain of inquiry (Systemwide Operations and Planning Advisory Group 2011). These teams, in turn, and on their own initiative, form specific task forces known as Lightning Teams. The structure is designed for responsiveness to problems and rapid solutions.

At the campus level, staff members at UCD technical services have been working on enterprise-level initiatives. To create capacity for these new initiatives and to address the challenges with shrinking staffing and increasing numbers of resources in electronic format, technical services first underwent a major reorganization in 2008. The two departments within technical services were restructured based on function rather than format. The new organization has enabled UCD technical services to develop new processes, streamline workflow, and engage in the library's outreach efforts.

One of the more notable changes UCD technical services made to contribute to systemwide efficiency took place in the newly formed Cataloging and Metadata Services department. All types of cataloging work were input into OCLC WorldCat directly, rather than simply into the library's local database. "We felt like the practice of editing a record in a library's own database doesn't make sense because if 100 libraries have that same title then every library has to do the same work if no one changes the record in the shared database. So why doesn't one cataloger enhance it in OCLC and benefit the rest of the 99 libraries? That's one reason we moved from the local to the networked level," says Xiaoli Li, head of Cataloging and Metadata Services. Making changes to OCLC master records requires catalogers to follow OCLC's input standards very closely. As a result, it can take longer for catalogers to edit the OCLC record than to modify the record locally. To maintain efficiency, the catalogers are adopting the new banner "good enough." This does not mean a reduction in quality, which would be inconsistent with OCLC. Rather, the idea is to target effort in the areas that can enhance the discovery of resources and omit those which have little or no impact. As Li explains, "In the past, people considered that the more complete a record is, the better quality it is, but I think that's a past practice," Li says. She continues, "It would be great if someone did some study, especially at the local level, to see what information is truly important to our patrons. That would be our guideline for doing cataloging. We have been practicing the concept of 'good enough' but without compromising the importance of discovery to our patrons." The emphasis on speed and responsiveness appears on the smaller scale of the cataloging department as well as the larger networked scale of the UC system.

In order to function more at the enterprise level, technical services reconfigured its entire workflow for processing PromptCat records (supplied by OCLC). Instead of manually examining every PromptCat record, a refined program was devised to identify "quality" records (Li 2012). The books represented by those records are sent directly to book labeling upon receipt. The automated process frees catalogers from routine cataloging work so they can devote more time to special collections. In addition, technical services redesigned its acquisitions process by using services provided by vendors as much as possible. One example was to set up EDI (electronic data interchange) for ordering and invoicing. Another example was moving work upstream by providing critical location information to vendors while placing orders. The information can then be used to create accurate holdings records and eliminate the need for manual intervention by acquisitions staff at the point of receiving physical books. All those enterprise-level changes have resulted in a significant amount of systematic efficiencies (Li 2012).

Technical services departments are also breaking the bounds that have traditionally excluded them from public service. One of the more recent goals of collection-building is the preservation and dissemination of university research through digitization. This initiative offers the means to circumvent the traditional route of peer-reviewed publishing and the problems that come with it, including backlog, copyright restrictions, and expense, all of which offer serious challenges to libraries and scholars. Technical services have played an important role in advising university researchers how to archive their information and make it available to digital networks. As indicated by its inclusion in the library strategic plan, this indeed could represent a future direction for technical services. Asked about the prediction that technical services staff would be absorbed into systems departments and essentially disappear, Li responds that there would no doubt be some benefit to centralizing technical services at the system level. This would include specialized language cataloging and electronic resources. But, she adds, "for certain activities, it does not make sense to centralize." These areas include the management of local specialized collections, "because they require a partnership with selectors who understand what resources are more important to describe in order to make them easily discoverable" (Li 2012). Other areas include the cataloging and preserving of documents on campus websites. This type of work requires an understanding of the context as well as copyright issues. "We are good at checking things and preservation issues, so I don't think that technical services will disappear from every campus" (Li 2012).

Under its new leadership, the UCD Library continues to try to bring its campus legacy of deep collections and a high level of service into a modern environment, while balancing the demands of the local with the UC system.

CASE STUDY TWO

::

University of California, Merced

A visitor to the University of California, Merced (UCM), described it as a landing site for spaceships: "There's nothing out there, and in the middle of nowhere you see these incredible buildings rising up." To paraphrase *The War of the Worlds*, "vast and cool intellects" indeed considered every facet of the founding of the university and its development plan. UCM, the tenth campus of the University of California, is a logical extension of the Master Plan of Higher Education, the blueprint that joins the UC system to the development of the state.

The site of the university, in the San Joaquin Valley, which occupies the southern half of California's Central Valley is the site of alarming demographic indicators: "The number of college graduates, the number of advanced-degree holders, and the number of young people attending the University of California is approximately half that of the rest of the state, while the per capita income is lower and other indicators of poverty are much higher than in the rest of the state" (Tomlinson-Keasey 2007, 17). Sequestered from the coast in the valley's dry environment, where temperatures routinely surpass 100 degrees in the summer, the small city of 80,000 and the surrounding region are pervaded by a sense of lassitude. The response from the state government was to build a university here that, like the other UC campuses, would inject money, business, and productivity into the region, providing its residents with assistance as well as the values of a first-rate education and, in turn, creating more contributors to the state in the new century. It is a testament to the strength of this vision that the project was completed despite the financial woes of California that preceded the national crash of 2008. These challenges, no doubt, helped to shape the original plan to make the first major university of the new century into an experiment in sustainability. From its very building plan to its recombination of academic disciplines into institutes for the study of sustainability, the new university aims to become a deep part of its region. Ironically, the newest member of UC takes its place next to what was philosophically the oldest, the University Farm that became UCD. Their locations are not far apart. UCD sits in the northern half of the Central Valley, just over two hours north-northwest by car from UCM. UCD, while retaining its expertise in the care of animals and crops, seeks to adapt its resources to new challenges. UCM, with its focus on sustainability, likewise constitutes a return to the land.

The construction of the UCM campus engaged with issues of sustainability from the outset. With the purchase of 10,000 acres, the initial building phase was planned for 2,000 acres. However, the U.S. Army Corps of Engineers discovered a rare form of fairy shrimp, a few centimeters in length, that inhabited vernal pools where buildings were sited for construction. Overall, the site provided potential habitat for as many as ten endangered or threatened species of plants and animals (Lollini 2012). The campus footprint was shifted and the building plan modified to accommodate the tiny creatures (Tomlinson-Keasey 2007, 22). The rest of the plan takes sustainability with utmost seriousness. Rather than as the mere preservation of the land (and the fairy shrimp), the campus defines sustainability in terms of an integration of buildings with the environment through a three-part definition. Every place depends on (1) space: the physical definition and sense of enclosure with all its textures; (2) activity: the social, cultural, and economic purposes of each space; and (3) path: the mode and speed of experiencing a space and activity (University of California, Merced, 2009, 65). The campus will become a living, dynamic part of the environment rather than building on top of it or preserving it as a specimen.

In the first phase of the campus, which is designed for 5,000 students, UCM's Kolligian Library plays a prominent role. Visitors entering the campus follow a long, rising road past student housing and support facilities to finally encounter the library as a sentinel that greets visitors while anchoring the front left (southwest) corner of the university quad. Indeed, because of limitations on space, the building currently houses much more than the library. The structure consists of two wings flanking a central edifice. The west wing, comprising three floors, is filled with administrative units. The central portion, the Lantern, houses a café with chairs and booths for eating and studying beneath a soaring ceiling. The east wing of four floors houses the library proper, but the ground floor is reserved for campus units whose offices open directly out onto the quad. Because of the multiple services built into the Kolligian Library, Donald Barclay, Interim University Librarian, observes that, at least for the first year of its operation, it was perhaps the only library in the country that could say that it has been used by every single student on campus (Barclay 2007, 110). Thomas Lollini, Campus Architect, adds, "You've got everyone on campus going in and out of the building with its various offices. Even the chancellor at the end of the day has to walk down through the students in the Lantern as she leaves the west wing" (Lollini 2012). The building participates in outreach.

By 2020, the campus hopes to double its enrollment to 10,000 students, and at some point in the future, to reach a maximum number of 25,000 students, putting it in the middle range of UC schools, comparable to UCD. In light of environmental considerations, campus development will move south, and the Kolligian Library will in effect rotate to the north end of campus about ten minutes away from the future center. At this point, according to Lollini, it may be time to construct a second facility to maintain the library's centrality. Thus, it will face the same concerns as UCD faces now in seeking to shift its physical center of gravity in a campus where the building plan is leaving the older structure on the margins. Meanwhile, Barclay speculates on other possibilities, such as "library-like spaces in different buildings around campus." At about 5,000 square feet each, these would contain technology, "whatever that would be," and "places for individual and group study." He adds, "My best guess is that the age of building a big building on campus just to hold books is over" (Barclay 2012). Such a vision looks even further back in history, to the departmental libraries that characterized the growth of the German research university model in America in the nineteenth century. But where such libraries were defined by their collections, the spaces envisioned by Barclay would dispense with physical collections and devote themselves to the learning process.

Let there be . . .

Light is the motif of the Kolligian Library. By night, the Lantern, with its suggestive cantilevered awnings, shines out on the quad as a central part of the campus lighting system. By day, the sunlight streams in through banks of broad windows. So abundant is the light that the library had to invest $40,000 to coat its windows in a film to protect the books. Extensive natural lighting contributes to the library's LEED gold certification, which is standard among all the buildings at UCM; other features include waterless urinals and solar power. Light is also a central element in the study space designed for students. Pale woods and matching colors reflect sunlight to make a cheerful, clean, pleasant environment. Tables and semi-enclosed study spaces fill the library floors, although as Barclay notes, the library dispensed with the barred carrels sometimes sought by graduate students (Barclay 2012). Curiously, the library's entry sequence harks back to the design of the first modern libraries of the nineteenth century by having its checkout desk and main service point on the second floor. (A student staffs an information desk on the first floor in the Lantern to refer queries.)

Apart from the location of the circulation desk, all similarities to older building designs cease. A staircase winds up from the second floor to overlook the circulation desk on one side while allowing one to peer through glass onto the floor of the Lantern on the other side. When observed during the summer, the Lantern was significantly more crowded than the library space although hardly distinguishable from it, as most tables had laptops open on them. The floor above the circulation desk is full of overhangs and unusual points of view. So where patrons of past libraries would find themselves floating among books that filled levels of translucent flooring, the users of the Kolligian Library find themselves floating in space among unusual perspectives as part of a new learning environment. One direction on the third floor leads to the periodicals room, directly above the Lantern. While there are uncataloged popular magazines to browse, the room is dominated by aquariums, tables, and sofas in green felt, and Lollini observes that the room functions as a place for students to mingle, lounge, and study in a version of a Learning Commons (Lollini 2012). Indeed, stertorous breathing emanated from one set of sofas during a visit, although its source remained invisible.

Barclay observes that libraries are like "public lands," with many different purposes (Barclay 2007, 106). Those interested in old-fashioned quiet can repair to the fourth floor above the periodicals room. The staff of the Kolligian Library does not enforce rules among patrons. But the fourth floor's quiet policy is maintained effectively by another aspect of the building's architecture. The transparent cantilevered structures that gird the Lantern on the outside are solid and opaque at this level, blocking much of the outside view with an impression of solid bars (fig. 12). One is not moved to make noise in this environment, and those who do are shushed quickly by other patrons. The east wing of the building is devoted to the library and is laid out more conventionally, with a modular floor

Fig. 12. A quiet area on the fourth floor of the Kolligian Library.

plan that has an identical layout from one floor to the other. A central staircase in the middle of each floor connects the floors to each other, and the floor space is divided among study areas and bookcases.

There are no signs. Barclay explains: "It is our belief that putting up a sign for the purpose of either telling someone where to go or how to behave is an admission that something is intrinsically wrong with the building or the information-seeking system" (Barclay 2007, 108). Eric Scott, Associate University Librarian for Library Operations, adds, "We hate signs here. Tacky" (Scott 2012). In their place, the building sports a profusion of large monitors, several mounted at strategic points on each floor, which display text and graphics on items of interest. The monitors also have speakers mounted in the ceiling that emit sound within a localized cone in the viewing area that will not disturb other patrons. If the UCM Library has read the future correctly, building design will play a large role in the operation of libraries.

The basic operational numbers for UC Merced as shown in table 3 are consistent with the profile of a new and thriving library. Generous shelf space is available. Operations show growth in all areas. The only irregularity is the high growth in ILL lending and transactions numbers relative to borrowing. This is atypical of a smaller physical collection, which one would expect to depend on larger libraries to supplement its holdings. The reasons for this irregularity are central to the achievements of UC Merced and are discussed below.

With the unique building design goes a singular vision of the staff who operate it. Budgetary pressures have reduced personnel to a mini-

Table 3. Vital Statistics, UC Merced Library, 2009–2010

Collection (4% to 531% change in last 5 years)	726,868
Circulation (–7.5% to 132% change in last 5 years)	74,268
ILL:	
Lending (69% to 250% change in last 5 years)	6,094
Borrowing (–8.3% to 74% change in last 5 years)	4,699
Shelf space occupied	44%
Reference transactions (35% to 169% change in last 3 years)	1,760
Instruction to groups (1% to 82% change in last 3 years)	177
Staff (0% change in last 2 years)	23
Budget (–1% to 20% change in last 5 years)	$2,970,364

Source: University of California Libraries 1992–2012 (UC Merced, with its commitment to smaller size as a design parameter for the future, falls outside of the collection requirements for ARL libraries and is not included in the official ARL Statistics. Data related to staff and shelf space obtained from UC Merced Library staff.).

Note: Parentheses indicate the highest and lowest rates of annual change in the preceding five years, not necessarily in order.

mum of twenty-one nonstudent staff. As a result, "every librarian is a manager," explains Barclay, and they supervise staff, including many highly trained students, for anything that does not require the librarian's expertise. To develop the cadre of librarians suited for UCM's unique mission, the library exercises care in its selection process. "We don't go out looking for people who are in our mold and are clones of us. But we do look for people who share values with us. . . . If your value is that I want to walk into a library with a big set of stacks and three million volumes so that I can browse through them, you're not going to be happy here" (Barclay 2012). Among its staff, the library cultivates vigorous debate. Building design plays a role here, too, since the staff mostly share adjacent offices on the second floor which allow them to communicate. "But," Barclay notes, "we also believe that once we decide to do things, we do them, and we don't tolerate people subverting what we're trying to do. I've been in libraries where that happens" (Barclay 2012).

In addition to its new building, the UCM Library represented a unique opportunity to design library services from scratch. In the beginning, "Bruce [Miller, founding University Librarian] had a Monte Carlo, and that's where we had our staff meetings," Barclay observes. "What we looked at were, 'What were things from the traditional library structure that we could use that still fit in our world? And what were the things that didn't fit anymore and we could get along without them?'" (Barclay 2012). A number of services taken for granted simply do not appear. "Reserve collections are a time-honored tradition in academic research libraries. We had no hesitation in tossing this tradition out on its ear" (Barclay 2007, 113). Print reserves, it is believed, are monopolized by a small number of users. Instead, documents are scanned into the campus courseware in a form of e-reserves to enable a version of the service.

There is also no ready reference collection. "People no longer come into the library looking for that kind of information," Barclay notes. Neither is there a food and drink policy, and patrons bring in whatever they wish. As for the danger to the collection? "People take books home and what do you think happens then?" asks Barclay. There are minimal technical services. The library relies entirely on shelf-ready materials for its book collection. Upon arrival, they are processed and shelved by one library staff person and student assistants. Thus, approximately twenty-five catalogers are reduced to one. In this incarnation of the future, technical services matches the more radical predictions for downsizing. The department spends the majority of its time manipulating files of bibliographic records for electronic resources. There are also no subject specialists. Apart from an approval plan that accounts for most of the collection, the library honors all faculty requests for materials. There are no workstations, except for a small set near the service desk on the second floor. When it opened, the library provided 200 laptops for checkout; these met student requirements for access, and their portability allowed students to take advantage of the different study environments in the building. The system worked well, but according to Barclay, when their replacement cycle was completed, it did not make sense to spend a quarter of a million dollars on equipment when most students had computer access anyway.

The library has no local OPAC. It was turned off in June 2012, and the library now relies entirely on Melvyl. Complaints have been negligible. The library's budget issues also differ from other UCs. While UCM has not suffered layoffs and collection cuts, "the library budget has not kept pace with the growth of the campus," according to Jim Dooley, head of Collection Services (Dooley 2012). "This is more insidious than journal collections, layoffs, closing branch libraries, etc.," he continues, "but none the less real. We may not need to draw down, but we do need increased funding to progress." With its efficient structure and forward-looking plans, the library seeks to make the most of a competitive budget environment.

Service

The services that the library does offer have survived a severe examination of their fitness and are subject to stringent and detailed assessment programs (UC Merced Library 2011; Abrams, Kunze, and Loy 2009; see also http://ucmercedlibrary.info/about-the-library/library-assessment-information). With reference as the library's sustained face toward its public, it will serve as a starting point for our review of services. The Kolligian Library has no central service desk staffed by librarians, and in its place relies on a robust system of referrals. A student at the information desk on the first floor responds to questions, as do students at the circulation desk on the second floor. In an extension of "roving reference," a cadre of red-shirted students, identified as reference assistants, roam about the library to provide help. Complex questions are referred to librarians. Sara Davidson, head of User Communication and Instruction, and Susan Mikkelsen, Resource Access and Instruction Librarian, have published the philosophy behind UCM's reference service (Davidson and Mikkelsen 2009). The reference service addresses the 80/20 division among reference questions, where the majority of questions do not require a librarian's expertise. These can be answered by the highly trained student staff. The library can thus reduce expenses with a smaller librarian staff, and librarians can manage their time more efficiently, spending more of it on appropriate tasks. Responding to calls in the profession for sophisticated reference instruction and a visible presence, Davidson notes, "I don't dispute the value of one-on-one interaction, but the reality is that we don't have the people to staff a desk eight hours a day." Mikkelsen adds, "There's all kinds of data that says that the majority of the questions that come in at a typical reference desk are not anything that has to be fielded by a librarian" (Mikkelsen 2012). The library's assessment plan calls for data on patron questions to be analyzed to ensure that roving staff levels are adequate.

While UCM's disciplines have a novel arrangement, into "thematic institutions," the library's instruction program for them follows a standard design. Most instruction takes the form of one-shot sessions requested by the yearlong writing sequence required of first-year UCM students. Students take an introductory writing course in the fall semester, followed by a second one in the spring based on an assessment of a portfolio. Higher level classes request instruction as needed. As of last year, the library has achieved its assessment goal of having 50 percent of writing students attend a library session. "I'm not sure we could handle much more anyway with the size of our staff," observes Teal Smith, User Communication and Instruction Librarian (T. Smith 2012). The instruction librarians continue to work at the problem of teaching information literacy, but they have high praise for LibGuides as multiplier of labor. The record shows a very high rate of use by students. "For a class of twenty-five, we will have 500 hits by the end of the semester," Smith notes. "The faculty eat them up," adds Mikkelsen. "They say, 'You mean you created this for our class?' They look very attractive and professional" (Mikkelsen 2012).

In addition to teaching the initial discovery steps required for information literacy, the instruction program, according to Barclay, seeks to move forward with the later stages of the process, especially source evaluation (Barclay 2007, 114). And this activity, central to final research papers, is another area that the library seeks to track through assessment. The university writing program currently has extensive surveys of students for its first-year sequence of courses. The library has managed to insert a small number of questions about library instruction into this effort thus far. Results indicate that the library sessions are well received. Assessment also indicates that while "students are much more likely to search web search engines" than library resources, "approximately 76% of students reported finding full-text articles through the UCM Library's online databases which they used for their Writing 10 papers" (Davidson 2011). Another report concludes, "Overall, the majority of the students (96.7%) appeared to use the library to help them in Writing 10 to complete at least one assignment" (Davidson 2012, 1). These are positive indicators of the library's relevance. On the other hand, the quality of the students' writing in the first year does not show significant improvement.

Whither Special Collections and Digitization?

Special collections is another area of innovation in the new library. Barclay observes, "It seemed to us that attempting to build a traditional special collection now is a bit like entering the Daytona 500 after all the other cars have a four-hundred-mile head start" (Barclay 2007, 112). Rather

than gathering new materials, the library has focused on digitizing existing collections to make them more accessible and without which they
would languish and accomplish little. To take one instance, Emily Lin,
head of Digital Assets, has digitized a collection of Japanese art from the
Clark Center for Japanese Art and Culture in Hanford, California (Lin
and Miller 2004). Documents were photographed with a high-quality
camera, and three-dimensional objects were reproduced by a process of
combining different two-dimensional images together. The public can access the digitized collection from the Online Archive of California (OAC),
part of the California Digital Library.

Along more traditional lines, the library has also been able to mount
an exhibit of local material as part of a collaborative project with Robin
DeLugan, an associate professor in the School of Social Sciences, Humanities, and Arts. DeLugan has undertaken to study the disadvantaged
population of the nearby Dos Palos region and to document the obstacles
to their progress. In addition to compiling demographic and economic
statistics, DeLugan's students conducted extensive fieldwork among the
people, which they recorded in their journals. These journals formed the
heart of the exhibit, according to Mary Weppler-Selear, former Library
Services Manager. "The journals are quite funny and poignant, really, the
whole gamut of emotions, quite beautiful" (Weppler-Selear 2012). The
journals, having been digitized, were put on a physical display during a library event and then sent out on loan to the Dos Palos community.
Whereas the library generally works indirectly through the university to
assist the local population, this project was one instance of direct
outreach.

With its small physical size, UCM is a vigorous participant in systemwide initiatives, and Lin, as chair of an NGTS task force, formalized
the library's goal of digitizing collections into a systemwide proposal (Lin
2010). Her report quantifies vast, backlogged special collections throughout the system that are inaccessible to most. She goes on to identify the
steps whereby the digitization of the Japanese collection that she accomplished could be extended into a model for the entire system. The ground-
work would need to be laid with a set of new directives and assumptions
for the system. First, the system would need a coordinated plan of acquisition whereby it decides which collections to digitize and distribute;
without this, the effort would be haphazard and inefficient. Secondly, the
system would need to adopt the MPLP (more product, less process)
guidelines for optimum efficiency. Finally, the various campuses would
need to adopt appropriate technology, such as the Archivists' Toolkit,

spearheaded by the UC San Diego Library, to speed up the work and to standardize output. Lin's report shows that the expenses and other requirements of the project are manageable.

Yet, for all its detail, this proposal has run into a challenge that is internal to the very large and complex advisory structure that the UC libraries use to identify issues and develop action plans. The board of the Systemwide Operations and Planning Advisory Group (SOPAG) oversees the Heads of Public Services (HOPS), the Heads of Technical Services (HOTS), All Campus Groups (ACGs), and Next Generation Technical Services (NGTS), which in many cases are heavily subdivided. The mass of information produced by these groups falls under the executive direction of the Council of University Librarians (CoUL) for the system. Originally CoUL, formed around 2008, served as a means for the ULs of the UC system to share information for mutual benefit. But such has been the success of this venture that information from SOPAG is now abundant, and the time has come to act and to commit time and resources. The decisions now facing CoUL have implications for the relationships between campuses and even for internal campus politics, and it remains to be seen how much the ULs can get their campuses to commit to systemwide efforts that may not have obvious and immediate benefits for them. Lin observes, "The way the CoUL works is dependent on the personalities as well as the mix of big campuses and small campuses. The members have to negotiate their own interests and systemwide interests" (Lin 2012). It would appear that libraries are now running into uncharted territory in large-scale administration of the kind suggestive of the Eurozone. Designed originally to facilitate logistical matters of convenience—open borders, shared currency, and so on—these matters turn out to have implications for sovereignty, autonomy, and hierarchy among the member nations that the existing governance structure is struggling to manage. So it is with the member institutions of the UC system. Along with other systemwide initiatives, the proposal to digitize collections waits upon the evolution of a decision-making apparatus.

In the meantime, priorities within UCM have shifted again. As Barclay puts it, "I thought, 'We're going to have this digital assets unit, and we're going to find cool stuff to digitize. But we can't just say the Merced irrigation district has 100 years of really cool records that might be good for research. And we spend all kinds of time trying to digitize them only to find out that nobody's interested in it. What we need to focus on is to help faculty manage their data" (Barclay 2012). Special collections has thus morphed into a new area that combines technology, outreach, and catalog-

in the UCM collection, all but 110,000 are electronic. But the number of electronic books does not represent a mere investment to be realized in the future, as appears to be the case with the Blaisdell Medical Library of UCD, where much of the electronic book collection remains unused. According to Dooley, there is heavy usage of e-books at UCM, and the investment in electronic books has paid off.

Such is the vitality of the UCM collection that it has produced an anomaly that one might call the UCM ILL mystery. One might suppose that for any given ILL network, such as the UC system, the lending rate of a library would be proportional to the size of its collection. Smaller collections will lend less and borrow more. Larger collections will lend more and borrow less. Indeed, there was a concern that UCM's smaller collection would be supported by larger institutions that would essentially be paying the bills for the material. But as of two years ago, UCM, with a collection approximately one-quarter the size of UCD's (and print material about one-thirtieth the size), is a net lender through ILL. Scott recalls, "The first time they gave me the report I couldn't believe it, and I told them to rerun it. 'There's something wrong.' But it was correct" (Scott 2012). The reasons for net lending remain unknown. Dooley suggests that the newness of the collection may be a factor. Given the 80/20 rule whereby only a fifth of a library's collection is used regularly, the elimination of older material in the collection reduces the level of nonuse and would tend to contribute to the vibrancy and interest of the collection; as books get older, their use plummets. Dooley also suggests that demand-driven acquisition models for e-books, where users have a limited number of views before the library must purchase the book, might play a role. "Essentially, [a system of short-term loans for e-books] is a supplement to ILL. If those short-term loans were translated into ILL requests for print books, you would see a huge difference in terms of borrowing versus lending. That again is why you see the interlibrary lending the way it is" (Dooley 2012).

Staff at UCM also have responses to Michael Gorman's questions about ILL and the shared collection model it supports. Gorman suggests that since the cost of ordering a book two or three times often equals the price of the book, ILL does not offer long-term savings. Scott answers, "What blows that equation out of the water is the cost of storing a book after purchase" (Scott 2012). UCM expects to remain active in ILL during the process of conversion to electronic materials.

UCM's collection, together with its ILL services, depends on the vision of a shared collection developed by the UC system, and Dooley has been in a position to observe this as a member and past chair of the UC libraries' Collection Development Committee and the ALCTS (Association for Library Collections and Technical Services) Acquisitions Section of ALA and as an original team member of NGTS who continues to work on cooperative collection development. He notes that for a time the system looked toward a model of centers of excellence, whereby a campus with a particular area of expertise would concentrate on that area and loan its materials to other campuses on demand. That method would cut down on duplication, which is the overriding goal of shared collections, and by locating collections in specific places, it would allow staff expertise to flourish there and add value to the materials. However, a plan that looks so efficient at the system level clashes with the responsibilities of the libraries to their campuses. It is hard to imagine how a collection that supports system-level demands in one area could fail to lose ground in other areas at the local level. And it is also questionable that ILL could satisfy local demand for everything outside of a library's designated areas of excellence (Dooley 2012).

Accordingly, interest is moving away from localized centers of excellence for print to packages of electronic materials that are available to the system as a whole. This indeed involves problems of its own, such as the extremely intricate structures of pricing that operate currently with serial packages and the technological and copyright issues now associated with electronic books. While Dooley maintains the value of economies of scale associated with subscription bundles, he reiterates the concerns of Lin about administrative structures at the system level to make timely decisions at this level of complexity. These complications only increase as UC reaches out to other shared repositories, a scenario destined to be repeated as networks proliferate among libraries. The potential problems can be glimpsed already in the fact that seven out of every ten HathiTrust records listed in Melvyl as electronic resources are not available for viewing. This is a situation decried unanimously by all Melvyl users but which has persisted for some time. As shared repositories are linked together, with their promises of efficiency and savings, the problems of sifting, prioritizing, connecting, and administrating must be dealt with as well.

Nevertheless, a process of subdivision is appearing, and the repositories are being recruited for specific contributions. The expertise of the HathiTrust, according to Dooley, is in electronic monographs and series with a capacity to expand its electronic archives of print monographs. Another repository in which UC participates is the Western Regional Storage Trust (WEST), which specializes in print serials. In this future vision with its contracts, costs, bottom lines, and mergers, driven largely by money, Dooley suggests that a key element for success may be rooted deeply in the tradition of libraries. "There is a certain level of trust that has to be built up. To an extent, the individual UC campuses have to trust the other UC campuses to act in everyone's best interest on a whole variety of issues . . . and when you expand it beyond UC to Hathi and WEST, you multiply the trust required, and you have to get into the idea that we are going to work together in a coordinated way and that we are going to trust each other" (Dooley 2012). Could it be that, at a time when libraries are being forced to conform to the pressures of the business world, the way to survive and thrive is through the values of service and idealism that have defined librarianship? Such a commitment to a systemwide vision also has implications for campus identities. According to Dooley, "One of R. Bruce Miller's ideas was that at UCM, our contribution was not going to be directly to the campus through our physical collection or the labor of our staff. It would lie in our contribution to the system that serves all the UCs" (Dooley 2012).

It remains to be seen whether UCM's high-speed approach to librarianship, which has radically changed library services and committed itself in new directions, is something that can be sustained as its successes are rewarded by further growth. Dooley may be right when he says that "over time the other UC libraries will begin to look more like us and we will look more like them" (Dooley 2012).

CASE STUDY THREE

⁚⁚

University of Hawai'i at Mānoa

The eight main islands that make up the state of Hawai'i constitute one of the most physically remote inhabited areas in the world. They were formed over geologic time scales by volcanic action as a magma hot spot on the floor of the central North Pacific pushed up through a sliding tectonic plate. The volcanoes that broke the surface of the water reached up into the trade winds that cross the ocean (and which powered the American clipper ships that operated a thriving trade in the nineteenth century). Loaded with evaporated moisture from their travels across the ocean, the winds form distinctive cumulus clouds as they climb the mountains of Hawai'i, releasing mists of rain to create the rainbows for which the islands are known. The rainfall then works its way through lava rock, creating spectacular waterfalls in the process, before percolating into reservoirs after a quarter-century journey as some of the purest water in the world. These natural processes created what Mark Twain called the "loveliest fleet of islands that lies anchored in any ocean," and Hawai'i continues to excite the imagination as a tropical paradise. But a location that appears remote and exotic also places Hawai'i in maximum proximity to the dynamic cultures of Oceania and the Asia-Pacific Rim, as witnessed by the history of the islands.

The islands were first discovered and settled beginning around AD 300 by voyagers from the Marquesas Islands and other points in Polynesia using navigation techniques of great sophistication that have only recently been recovered by the Polynesian Voyaging Society. Over time, these peoples formed the rich and intensely religious culture of ancient Hawai'i. Western contact by the British explorer James Cook in 1778 closely coincided with the first-ever unification of all eight islands into a single kingdom by Kamehameha I. Hawai'i maintained a monarchy in the nineteenth century, modeled along European lines and featuring extensive travel by its members throughout the world. Hawai'i even participated in the Great Game of political alliances in the nineteenth century to the extent of ejecting the Russians in their attempts to build a fort and developing formal relationships with other Western powers. In addition to the commercial port of Honolulu with its value for trade, the United States took an interest in Pearl Harbor as a base to offset the projected ambitions of Imperial Japan, which had been recently opened to the world by Commodore Perry of the U.S. Navy (Dukas 2004). Such foresight nevertheless failed to prevent the Day of Infamy decades later, when the Japanese attacked Pearl Harbor on December 7, 1941. In the interim, American owners of sugar and pineapple plantations brought Japanese and Chinese laborers to the islands, where they produced these signature exports and formed a vital part of the new island culture. In 1893, American businessmen, with the aid of U.S. Marines, deposed the Hawai'ian monarchy and claimed the islands as a territory for the United States, an act that remains a source of political controversy and activism within the Native Hawai'ian community. Today, attendants on flights from Asia describe Honolulu International Airport as the "gateway to the United States," while the United States looks outwards from Hawai'i to new political developments in Asia in the twenty-first century. Despite its seeming isolation, Hawai'i has always been connected to the Pacific through lines of geopolitical force and information. A university with a library for the gathering of knowledge was a natural development. In the context of libraries, the University of Hawai'i at Mānoa (UHM) is a meditation on the importance of place.

Sea, Land, Space

UHM was established in 1907 on the island of O'ahu in the tradition of land grant universities by the Second Morrill Act. Operating out of its first building, Hawai'i Hall, the university served as an agricultural institution for the first half century of its existence. The current strategic plan for 2011–2015 updates the original mission of the university to a sea, space, and land grant institution that ranks among the top thirty recipients of extramural research grants in the United States (University of Hawai'i at Mānoa 2011, 7). The university's long-range development plan also looks to restore some of the islands' history (University of Hawai'i at Mānoa 2007). For example, the main campus in the Mānoa valley sits in one of the *ahupua'a* of old Hawai'i. These wedge-shaped slices of land expanded from points in the central mountain ranges down to the sea. As a result, each ahupua'a contained the full variety of Hawai'ian terrain with its fertile valleys and drier coastal plains, a complete ecosystem that could support independent communities that served as the basis of the ancient Hawaiʻian social system. The university's historical ahupuaʻa has the distinction of including the Waikīkī district favored by the class of chiefs (aliʻi) and now developed into the major district for tourism that supports Hawaiʻi's economy. *The Chronicle of Higher Education*, quoted in a university brochure, describes UHM as "the most diverse college campus in the United States" (University of Hawaiʻi at Mānoa 2008).

Steve Meder, Assistant Vice Chancellor for Physical, Environmental, and Long Range Planning, explains that the university is actively investigating environmental issues that affect the state as a whole (Meder 2012). Research is under way to understand the details of precipitation in the valley and the movement of water. With its current population load, the spectacular waterfalls of Hawaiʻi are drying up, and UHM seeks models for better ways to use rainfall and to recharge the aquifers. "We have some of the best researchers in the country here and highly talented students. We try to work with these groups to apply their work to solution-based approaches to campus problems, and I think it's an approach that is unique," observes Meder. UHM also pursues research in other areas of sustainability. Electricity (because of the transport of oil) is enormously expensive, at 36 cents per kilowatt-hour as opposed to 6 cents on the Mainland. "All the university buildings are required to meet an LEED certification of silver, but that's not good enough for us," notes Meder. As part of the revitalization of the campus, plans are under way to convert it from a commuter to an urban campus. This will be done in part through transportation incentives to encourage the university community to ride the city's award-winning bus system as well as modifications to make the campus more walkable and bike-friendly. Varney Circle, a roundabout adjacent to Hawaiʻi Hall and the university's original quad, will serve as the organizational heart of the future campus. But the campus will operate more as a set of decentralized nodes, consisting of community spaces linked by tree-shaded walks and bike paths. The university calls upon historical tradition to pursue sustainability.

The current library consists of two buildings that occupy two such community spaces. The Gregg M. Sinclair Library, built in 1956, arises from a network of paths among a grove of trees near the main entrance of the campus. Amid the robust period of library growth in the 1960s and a prosperous Hawaiʻi economy at the time, the university constructed a second library building only a decade later. The Thomas Hale Hamilton Library sits on the opposite side of campus, anchoring one end of McCarthy Mall, a scenic walkway overhung with trees.

The figures in table 4 show how the UHM Library has worked to maintain its services against a static budget. The major budget crisis for

**Table 4. Vital Statistics, University of Hawai'i at Mānoa
Library, 2009–2010**

Collection (–2% to –14% change in last 5 years)	3,602,058
Circulation (–4.6% to –14% change in last 2 years)	368,869
ILL:	
Lending (9.5% to 12.6% change in last 2 years)	7,707
Borrowing (9.5% to 24% change in last 5 years)	27,943
Shelf space occupied	N/A
Reference transactions (6% to –20% change in last 5 years)	38,670
Instruction to groups (2.3% to 56% change in last 5 years)	663
Staff (–7.5% to 16% change in last 5 years)	237
Budget (–8.5% to 7.8% change in last 2 years)	$17,455,232

Source: Official ARL Statistics (Kyrillidou and Bland 2008, 2009; Kyrillidou
and Morris 2011; Kyrillidou, Morris, and Roebuck 2011; Kyrillidou and
Young 2008).

Note: Parentheses indicate the highest and lowest rates of annual change
in the years indicated, not necessarily in order.

the university and the state took place in the 1990s as a result of a confluence of factors that included the "bursting of the Japanese prosperity
bubble," the First Gulf War, and Hurricane Iniki. Recovery came about
through a "structural transition from an aging, sun-and-surf tourist destination to a diversified and technology-savvy economy for the 21st century" (Naya 2000, 5; Cayetano 2000, 10). In the new millennium, the
university's budget has failed to match inflation but neither has it suffered severely.

Student Success

With the construction of Hamilton Library, Sinclair was converted to
the undergraduate library while Hamilton became the graduate library.

Over time, Sinclair began to incorporate instructional technology. Paula Mochida, former head of Sinclair Library (1982–1987) and Interim University Librarian (2007–2011), established the Wong Audiovisual Center in 1986 by combining a media center with a then separate film unit and seeking sponsorship from Harry C. and Nee-Chang Wong. In 1988, Mochida worked with David Lassner, then Assistant Director of Computing Services, to establish the Computer Learning and Information Center, a 100-station computer and CD-ROM LAN (local area network) in the library. It was the largest such center on campus and probably one of the largest of its kind in existence at the time. In 2006, the space was revitalized again under the direction of then head of Sinclair Library Gregg Geary with the creation of a Learning Commons. The bottom floor where it is located has evolved into a truly modern facility with large, airy open spaces. Immense louvered windows, which occupy much of the wall space on the mountainside (*mauka*), transmit trade winds into spacious, high-ceilinged reading rooms equipped with open tables and armchairs. Sitting in these chairs amidst the breeze, a visitor can pass a gratifying stretch of time while doing nothing at all.

Upon entering the building, one encounters an information concierge desk with staff to direct visitors to the many services and amenities of the Student Success Center, as the commons is known. These include a room full of rows of half carrels, each equipped with power outlets, which have proven to be extremely popular. "The students absolutely love that," says Melissa Arakawa, Education Specialist and manager of the Success Center (Arakawa 2012). Nearby are three group study rooms, each featuring a large table, widescreen TV with projector and DVD player, and a whiteboard where students can practice presentations. Another especially popular service, according to Arakawa, is proctoring of exams. Also on the ground floor is the Wong Computer Lab and Digital Media Studio, funded by the same patrons of the Audiovisual Center on the third floor. In addition to an extensive suite of software for the many workstations, the studio features equipment for digitizing musical recordings, and this capability will be extended in the future by walling off a section of the lab and adding technology to complement the Wong Audiovisual Center. "Since it's a music library, they want to build stations with recording software on them that people can hook up to their guitars and amps," says Arakawa.

But perhaps the crowning achievement of the Student Success Center is to have gathered together advising offices from around campus. "What we've seen and what our patrons have told us is that they go to places within the university and say, 'I'm looking for something about advising,' and they get passed around the campus. We saw that need, and we strive to be a referral service about anything that a student has a question about" (Arakawa 2012). These services include a Learning Assistance Center, a peer-tutoring service, the office of the first-year seminar, and the Honors Program within steps of each other and the computer lab. (The peer-tutoring service has since relocated most of its services to its main office but continues to negotiate with the Student Success Center to find an optimal location.) The upper floors house outreach programs in the form of the P-20 program, which coordinates the entire state's educational efforts from primary through graduate school, and the Outreach College, which offers night classes to the community. The Student Success Center has realized the Learning Commons ideal by combining lounge areas, educational technology, and assistance into a versatile, creative space.

The achievements of the Success Center have been extensively documented, largely through questionnaires administered to users. "The one thing that we've noticed that stands out to us is that the foot traffic in the library has increased tenfold" (Arakawa 2012). The average during the middle of the day has risen to about 300 to 400 students. During finals, the library is open 24/7 for most of the week and often fills its 800 seats to capacity. There is evidence of cross-referrals among the different offices housed in the building. "One of the bigger ones is between the library and our first-year programs" (Arakawa 2012). First-year seminars are held in Sinclair, with plenty of opportunity for instruction. "We're introducing the freshmen early to what the library offers. . . . The first-year program shares its data with us, and the students absolutely love to know what's going on," adds Arakawa. While looking to the future in instructional design, the Student Success Center also maintains continuity with the past. Mochida observes, "Actually in talking and building the concept, some of us old-timers were going, 'Gosh this is really reminiscent of the undergraduate library.' . . . Lots of teaching and showing students where to go; they've brought many of those services together" (Mochida 2012).

Into the Twenty-First Century

Constructed in 1968 (with additions added in 1987 and 1999), Hamilton Library opens into a lobby with low ceilings that differ from the vast monumental spaces of some libraries, but a gorgeous mural by Juliet May

Fraser brightens the area with an ancient Hawai'ian scene. And while the ceilings prevent upward expansion, the library opens horizontally outward onto a mall. A large glassed-in area is set aside with tables and chairs for studying. This area is under consideration for a "Research Commons" that would complement Sinclair Library or be merged outward into a communal space with the Paradise Palms food court across a walk (fig. 13). The basic design of Hamilton corresponds to a modular plan with essentially identical layouts on each floor. Various departments such as the Asia Collection and the Hawai'ian and Pacific Collections have their own reading rooms and reference desks in the building (fourth and fifth floors, respectively). An addition, reachable via an enclosed bridge from the first and second floors, houses the Science and Technology Collection on the lower levels and the Preservation Department, Rare Books, and University Archives on the fifth floor.

A visitor to Hamilton Library encounters the Business, Humanities, and Social Science reference desk in a large open space on the first floor not unlike the location of the UCD reference desk in its most recent configuration. This desk is staffed by reference librarians and students from the UHM Library and Information Science (LIS) program housed in the basement and serves as the de facto general reference desk for the building. The library has made a presence in new technologies of outreach but has not decided where to invest further. The library's one QR code currently points to its main web page. Enabling access to the website through mobile devices is easier than getting patrons to actually use it, according to Martha Chantiny, head of Desktop Network Services (Chantiny 2012). The library has also acquired a large-screen TV located in the addition that is used for exhibits.

UHM has, however, made significant process in the area of scholarly communication with its institutional repositories. After a period of exploration through pilot programs, the library has experienced such demand that it now hosts three separate repositories. ScholarSpace stores the research and data of faculty, according to Beth Tillinghast, a librarian for Desktop Network Services. eVols stores items over which UHM has stewardship but which are not publications of UHM faculty. The UH System Repository stores research for faculty in other campuses in the system (currently two other campuses are participating). In spring 2012, an open access policy was endorsed by the UHM faculty senate and approved by the chancellor allowing faculty to deposit copies of their research in institutional repositories (University of Hawai'i at Mānoa Library 2012). (Faculty can opt out.) The UHM policy is one of the few

Fig. 13. Communal space between Hamilton Library (left) and an adjoining food court.

that operates at a campus level as opposed to within departments or schools. As part of the newly formed Coalition of Open Access Policy Institutions led by the University of Kansas, UHM intends to continue a leadership role in the open access publishing movement (Mochida 2012).

Science and Technology and Public Services librarian Sara Rutter and her colleagues have undertaken workshops around campus to inform faculty of the repository service and its benefits. In addition to the open access policy, they have been aided by the recent requirement of the National Science Foundation that grant applications contain a data management plan; this has had a powerful effect on a university with a high number of scientific grants. In practice, the librarians end up working less with faculty than with graduate students, who are both motivated and capable enough to learn data management skills (Rutter 2012). The repositories use DSpace, and its Dublin Core metadata has proven adequate for most patrons.

While the librarians have worked with social scientists, much of the emphasis remains on scientific work. In a reflection of librarianship as a whole, the humanities have not participated in the technological innovations of the repository at the same rate as scientists. Kate Lingley, an associate professor of art history with a specialty in Chinese culture, not only works in a second language but must also deal with extensive copyright issues for publication of images. She is not yet ready to invest effort in a scholarly repository. "It takes so much work for me to produce an article. It's really hard to imagine putting it in a repository where someone's going to say this isn't peer-reviewed—where someone's going to write it off for not being peer-reviewed" (Lingley 2012). Though robust, the institutional repository program remains devoted largely to the sciences and the social sciences. In addition to its three repositories, the data management effort at UHM has benefited from a series of circumstances.

The Great Flood

The water in the Mānoa valley that is under study by environmental planners made its presence known in 2004 with a damaging flood. A flood control channel in the surrounding mountains became obstructed and overflowed after more than forty days of continuous rain, and muddy water cut a vast swath across campus. While it made a huge mess and caused significant damage, the flood reserved special fury for Hamilton Library. A light well in the shape of a moat around the building trapped the water, allowing it to build up pressure until it exploded forcefully inward. A three-inch-thick steel door buckled, according to Chantiny (Chantiny 2012). Under this pressure, the water surged through the lower level, annihilating everything and forcing LIS students to break a window and make their escape out of the other side of the building. Almost the entire government documents and maps collections were rendered unusable.

After eight years, the facility has been restored. FEMA paid for the damage to be bulldozed and equipment to be replaced. Belfor Property Restoration, a disaster recovery firm, restored some of the maps collection. About 80 percent of the government documents have been replaced, partly through donations from other libraries. After years of displacement, the library staff has moved back into permanent quarters. Yet the university took a lesson from this disaster, and its determination to safeguard its records from future natural disasters helped to drive plans for a new information technology building. The building is currently under construction and will be the premier data center in the state, according to Gwen Jacobs, interim head of Cyberinfrastructure at UHM (and a professor of neuroscience visiting from Montana State University) (Jacobs 2012). The IT center itself is just one part of a more comprehensive plan for infrastructure.

Currently the priority is to establish hardware and connectivity. "UHM faces unusual challenges because of its location. . . . Cables have to be laid on the ocean floor to connect the islands," notes Jacobs. But in building hardware, the cyberinfrastructure effort faces constraints to minimize cost and preserve a green campus. "Power is a basic constraint here," says Jacobs, no doubt due to the high costs of electricity on the islands. In response, the cyberinfrastructure effort seeks economies of scale by coordinating machines rather than buying new ones. For the final vision, integrating technology and staff, Jacobs explains, "We want to go from a scientist who sets up lab space, buys a computer, and plugs it into a wall and says, 'Now what?' to being able to set up campus IT to be able to provide services for them."

Currently, the library is operating independently of IT, but as the repository program grows, the library will look to campus IT for archiving and other needs that will become more apparent as the infrastructure takes shape. "What I'd like to build is a whole consulting service like a research computing group except that their jobs are to talk to people, to help them" (Rutter 2012). The staff would be drawn from the computer science discipline. For its part, the cyberinfrastructure group is not yet sure how it will use the library's expertise. "What will really help is some study that shows that the success of grant applications depends on the quality of the data management plan," says Jacobs. "So far, we have nothing. It's like the Wild West out there."

The "Special" Area Collections

In addition to the sciences, especially those having to do with biology and marine and tropical environments, UHM possesses a unique excellence in its area studies of Hawai'i, Asia, and the Pacific. The Hawai'ian Collection is the original special collection of Hamilton Library. (The University Archives and Rare Books departments are located separately in the building's new addition.) Yet the other area collections are so robust and vital as to function almost as special collections in their own right. One might suppose that these collections appeared in the post–World War II era with the rise of area studies throughout the profession. That narrative describes the East-West Center, established in 1960. Located fairly near Hamilton Library, the center consists of several dormitories, a convention center, another building for classrooms and administration, and Lincoln Hall, a hotel. The overlap with the library's area studies is evident in what is sometimes referred to as a "midnight raid" (1961), when the East-West Center physically removed what was then known as the collection of the Oriental Institute from Sinclair Library to its own facility. The material was subsequently returned and collection policies developed by the East-West Center to complement the library holdings. While the center currently contributes some funds to the library's collections, its interests are confined largely to politics, business, and current events. The area studies collections stem from an older tradition rooted in the large number of Asia-focused courses taught at UHM and, ultimately, in the diverse population of the islands. Professors of Chinese and Japanese occupied faculty positions at the founding of the university in 1907. A Hawai'ian collection of 350 books was represented in the library's original holdings out of a desire to gather material on Hawai'iana. (I am indebted to Jim Cartwright, Martha Chantiny, and Patricia Polansky for providing historical background on the university.) Gregg M. Sinclair, future university president (1942–1955), established the Oriental Institute in 1935, almost a quarter of a century prior to the founding of the East-West Center. This tradition synergized with newer departments for the Pacific, Southeast Asia, the Philippines, Korea, and Russia in their development of eminent collections.

The activities of the Hawai'ian and Pacific Collections and the Asia Collection are too extensive and varied to cover in detail, but they share a number of features. Occupying the fourth floor, the Asia Collection librarians use a common reference desk and reading area while the Hawai'ian and Pacific Collections share similar facilities on the fifth floor. All three collections attract the interest of large numbers of researchers on both sides of the Pacific. The librarians typically undertake annual acquisition trips to sometimes remote locations (Guadalcanal and New Guinea as well as Taiwan, Japan, and Russia) to gather materials and maintain professional relationships; some collections operate perpetual exchanges of material with partner institutions. In their relations to the university, the departments go far beyond the usual liaison role of libraries. Each librarian interacts with a disciplinary center as well as with single departments and individuals. These centers are higher level administrative units that help to coordinate researchers of different academic departments such as history, anthropology, linguistics, and sociology, as well as the relevant language departments. Some centers have elaborate physical facilities of their own that include classrooms, administrative space, and lecture halls, but all operate to coordinate research, instruction, and promotional activities for their members. In addition to assisting publication by faculty fellows, some centers produce entire publications of their own, such as *The Contemporary Pacific*, the journal of the Center for Pacific Islands Studies. The centers also typically undertake grant-writing activities, which include but are not limited to renewable grants from the U.S. Department of Education's National Resource Centers.

The integrative work of the centers provides another instance of Boyd's rapid decision cycling that area studies librarians have used to advantage. With long-standing relationships and, in some cases, seats on executive boards, the librarians network with great efficiency among the faculty fellows to learn about their work, support them with collection-building, and provide specialized instruction. By working on the editorial boards of journals produced by the centers, the area bibliographers have already surpassed roles in scholarly communication that other libraries have just begun to formulate. The centers have also allowed the area librarians to become managers in the way described by Donald Barclay at Merced. Japan studies librarian Tokiko Bazzell often exhibits material in the library and coordinates symposia in collaboration with the Center for Japanese Studies (Bazzell 2012). "These events can sometimes help to gain more grants," Bazzell says. China studies librarian Kuang-Tien Yao has applied her training in cataloging to develop a new procedure whereby vendors in China provide a MARC record to speed up the acquisition of materials requested by faculty. This procedure has been adopted by other members of the Council on East Asian Libraries, an organization that spans North America. The faculty of the various centers are enthusiastic in their praises of their area librarians. Lingley, who holds a position on the executive board of the Center for Chinese Studies, observes, "KT [Kuang-Tien] has been very creative in using little pockets of money that are donated" to purchase a $3,000 reference on Chinese Buddhist sculpture. "I would never have been able to buy that for myself" (Lingley 2012). Philippine specialist Elena Maria Clariza is also an executive committee member at the Center for Philippine Studies, and she teaches an online course that includes students in the Philippines. "I view it as giving back to the areas that provide us with material" (Clariza 2012). She is also constructing an online education site on the Philippines that has been used by public schools in Chicago since the fall of 2012.

The Hawai'i and Pacific Collections are world renowned. The steady addition of Pacific-area materials to the original Hawai'ian Collection led to the recruitment in 1969 of Renée Heyum, Pacific bibliographer at the Musée de l'Homme in France. Heyum created the outlines of the Pacific Collection as it exists today, according to Lynette Furuhashi, retired Pacific specialist (Furuhashi 2012). With support from the Center for Pacific Islands Studies, Heyum initiated annual trips to the Pacific to acquire government documents, local and indigenous publications, and other unique materials, and she helped to found *The Contemporary Pacific*. Her efforts were recognized with France's highest award for civilians in 1993. Heyum was followed in her role as curator of the Pacific Collection by Karen Peacock, who led the department until her passing in 2010. (For a sensitive account of Peacock's accomplishments and those of the staff of the Pacific Collection, see Dawrs 2010–2011.) In addition to continuing to build the collection, Peacock helped to develop a grant to educate librarians from the Pacific Region, a program that continues under the direction of PREL (Pacific Resources for Education and Learning) and the University of North Texas. As with the other area departments, the work of the Pacific Collection is carried out by an exceptionally dedicated and energetic staff with a sense of mission. "We want to work in this collection because it's an amazing resource. . . . We are beholden to the entire world in that we are the defining collections of these regions. I think all of us hold a very strong sense of responsibility both to the collection and the people we serve," explains Pacific specialist Eleanor Kleiber. The multiple achievements of the Pacific Collection, which include innovative staffing, education, data collection, and community building at an international level, are paradigm shifting. Mingling tradition with the most advanced ideas across the full spectrum of library-related issues, the UHM experience suggests that traditional library practices have a far richer potential than predicted by even the most ambitious projections for the future.

Librarianship and the Sacred

Cultural preservation at UHM extends to a new area of the profession known as indigenous librarianship. Devoted to the preservation of indigenous cultures, this field also questions the most basic assumptions of modern librarianship. Among the uncertainties facing the profession, most librarians would agree on the importance of technology and individual access as foundational principles. Yet indigenous librarians point to history for an alternative view. (This summary of indigenous librarianship is indebted to the writing of Loriene Roy; see Roy and Hogan 2010, 125; Roy 2009; Roy and Cherian 2004.) At the center of the public library movement in the nineteenth century was an effort to assimilate immigrants and newcomers into the expanding United States. While libraries clearly worked to the advantage of many newcomers from foreign shores, they played a somewhat different role in the vigorous reeducation efforts aimed at Native Americans. These had dubious results for assimilation and, as has been only recently appreciated, traumatic and destructive effects on native cultures and people. Librarians today who celebrate diversity like to think that the mistakes of the past have been rectified, yet the past may not be so far removed. In a modern incarnation of utilitarianism, indigenous collections are marginalized in the quest to improve both bottom line and usage statistics. Even when successfully executed, the extraction of certain kinds of cultural knowledge from their contexts constitutes a violation of its own. Some Native American stories were meant to be told only in certain seasons, and sacred information was sometimes restricted to particular individuals (Roy and Hogan 2010, 127). For these cultures, the ethic of individual access becomes a threat. In stripping away the cultural context of information with indiscriminate technological access, libraries may be destroying the very thing they set out to preserve. The case is reminiscent of the archaeologist Heinrich Schliemann, excavator of the legendary city of Troy, who, in his eagerness to delve into the depths of his site, ended up destroying layers of valuable artifacts along the way. While restrictions on technology and access sound strange to librarians, the concept is more familiar than first appears. Librarians have resisted the Patriot Act as part of their mission to safeguard the privacy of their patrons. So the withholding of information for the sake of higher principles of education is already part of library practice today. Librarianship can learn from the past in the traditions of indigenous culture as well as peer into the future.

Kuleana (Accountability), ʻOhana (Family), Ahupuaʻa (Sustainability)

The School of Hawaiʻian Knowledge, Hawaiʻinuiākea, has a striking presence, with modern buildings whose soaring roofs represent the architecture of traditional *kauhale* (houses). Extending partially under a bridge for a campus thoroughfare, the school rests within centuries-old irrigation streams that originate in the interior of Mānoa valley.

Shanye Valeho-Novikoff, librarian of the Hālau o Laka me Lono Resource Center at Hawaiʻinuiākea, observes that the original deeper meaning of ahupuaʻa is not only about geographic boundaries but also about the principle of sustainability (*malama ʻaina*), which is one area of concentration at the school (Valeho-Novikoff 2012). Hawaiʻinuiākea comprises four divisions: Kamakakūokalani Center for Hawaiʻian Studies, Kawaihuelani Center for Hawaiʻian Language, Ka Papa Loʻi O Kānewai Cultural Garden (for the study of traditional crafts), and the Kauhale (Native Hawaiʻian Student Services). Besides a traditional academic focus similar to other area studies centers, Hawaiʻinuiākea has also pursued a broader agenda to preserve indigenous knowledge. The curriculum offers classes on fiber arts, printmaking, resource management, Hawaiʻian astronomy, Hawaiʻian medicinal herbs, and much more. The cultural garden contains working taro patches fed by historical irrigation streams to teach ancient agricultural techniques.

The taro plant is more than the source of poi, the staple of the traditional Hawaiʻian diet; it is the basis of a whole cosmology, linking the people to the land, and to the divine (Holmes 2000, 45). The root of the kalo plant, as taro is called in Hawaiʻian, may also give its name to ʻohana, the Hawaiʻian word for family. The concept denotes a more extended structure than Western models; its members are bound less by strict roles than by a powerful communal ethic. The taro patches of the cultural garden thus constitute a working symbol of the integrated education at Hawai'inuiākea, and in this spirit the school offers extensive outreach programs to the Hawai'ian community and makes its facilities available after working hours. The varied landscape of the school, with its distinctive roofs, low-lying cultural garden, and open spaces, merges seamlessly into its varied activities.

The specialized curriculum at Hawai'inuiākea not only supports basic research into Hawai'ian culture but also provides a foundation for professional training. The school grants bachelor's and master's degrees and is actively involved in the ongoing struggle of the Hawai'ian people for political recognition. After the founding of the Center for Hawai'ian Studies in 1987, the organization was, for a time, involved in political activism. This has changed, says Valeho-Novikoff, into a model where the school produces graduates, imbued with a deep appreciation of Hawai'ian culture, who can enter professional careers and take a direct role in shaping the future of Hawai'i (Valeho-Novikoff 2012). To accomplish these goals, Hawai'inuiākea draws on the world-famous Hawai'ian collection at Hamilton Library as well as its embedded Resource Center. The center comprises a large room staffed by Valeho-Novikoff. Reference service has no boundaries, as the librarian fields questions at any time, and instruction is done at the request of faculty without a formal schedule. Otherwise, the center has integrated itself into the activities of Hawai'inuiākea as it charts a new path in indigenous studies. The center's print collection is divided into three categories—Hawai'i, the Pacific, and the Americas—to facilitate cross-cultural study. The Hawai'ian section includes extensive records of the land to support the major requirements and areas of concentrations such as Kūkulu Aupuni (Envisioning the Nation), Mālama 'Āina (Resource Management), and Mo'olelo 'Ōiwi (Native History and Literature). The librarians also compile tapes of classical spoken Hawai'ian made by *kūpuna* (elders) with distinctive pronunciation to help preserve and disseminate the language (a major issue of indigenous librarianship). Technology is not neglected in the study of tradition, and construction is under way of an online Knowledge Well that will include multimedia records of traditional lore and practices. "The collection," writes Valeho-Novikoff, "strives for the interconnectedness of all knowledge, contemporary and ancestral, from Kanaka Maoli (Native Hawai'ian) perspectives in order that students will understand Kanaka Maoli experiences in the context of world indigenous peoples." The vision here of integrated knowledge cultivated with different learning styles—

tactile, experiential, participatory, and collective—suggests that the Learning Commons at Sinclair Library has roots that go back past the former Undergraduate Library to the ancient Hawai'ian culture, which anticipated modern developments in education.

Creation and Destruction

The faithful preservation of culture is a clear goal for indigenous librarians, but its principles may extend further into the main currents of the profession. A critique of utilitarianism appears in the objections of David Michalski, UCD librarian, to features of the UC system's Melvyl interface. The vast and undifferentiated results, he claims, "don't respect the collection that we have been building for our users for the last sixty years" (Michalski 2012). Perhaps we are all indigenous librarians in the face of shared collections. The tension between centralization, driven by financial and technical forces, and specialized collections, anchored in more traditional values of preservation, is inherent in the changes that the profession finds itself confronting now. This tension is manifesting itself in the internal organization of the UHM Library. A report by R2 Consulting, commissioned by Mochida, outlines the issues. The library, according to the report, has a high degree of professionalism in their staff and outstanding materials in their collections, but the organization is coping with disarray (R2 Consulting LCC 2009, 4). Much of this comes from external circumstances. UHM did not have an official University Librarian from 2006 to 2013 (when Irene Herold was appointed), and the Interim University Librarian during that time, Mochida, retired in 2011. Because of fluctuation at the top, the library has had to draw during that period on department-level talent for its administration, leaving the various departments without regular means of communication with each other (R2 Consulting LCC 2009, 5). Russian bibliographer Patricia Polansky, who has completed forty-two years at UHM, suggests that the delay in recruiting a University Librarian may have been related to the university's focus on science (Polansky 2012). There have been other external disruptions. While the material damage from the flood of 2004 was being repaired, staff members were removed to temporary quarters for as long as five years, disturbing the cohesiveness of the library.

Against this backdrop, R2 focused on problems with technical services, many of which are rooted in the current library organization. The many outstanding collections of the library operate with an extensive backlog. This results from delays in the acquisitions department (some of which resulted from the flood) and from the specialized requirements of the area studies collections. R2 questioned whether the departmental organization could be streamlined. In particular, it suggested that the government documents department might consider removing itself from the Federal Depository Library Program and replacing print items with electronic as much as possible. R2 also questioned the intermediate status of the library's large Asia Collection, proposing that the Hawaiʻi and Pacific Collections alone retain the designation of a special collection in order to save time in processing materials. In terms of the technical services operation itself, R2 very much looked to the future, arguing for standardized cataloging based on the "good enough" norms, shelf-ready cataloging, and the use of e-resources to replace print.

Gwen Sinclair, government documents librarian, says that the reception to the R2 report was generally positive and the sense was that "they got it right" (Sinclair 2012). Amy Carlson, head of Serials and interim head of Collection Services, says that many of the report recommendations for acquisitions have been completed, and cataloging is now working on the details of appropriate "good enough" standards. However, exception was taken to the department recommendations. Sinclair observes that UHM is a regional repository that is unique in the state and important for the state government as well as university scholars. The massive digitization of federal documents under way does not cover many valuable elements of the collection, especially the older material. Similarly, Carlson remarks that R2 didn't fully understand the role of the Asia Collection: "They pull in a lot of grant money with the NRC; they serve the whole university" (Carlson 2012). Japan specialist Bazzell, responding to comments about usage, says, "When I find a book that someone really needs for scholarship, it is just amazing to me that this knowledge has been preserved, and it shouldn't be given up" (Bazzell 2012). The differences with R2 are more a matter of values than numbers. Indeed, the usage metric applied in isolation would seem to punish the Asia Collection for the very uniqueness which is at the heart of its value.

The UHM Library was encouraged by the R2 report to undertake an even larger reorganization. Budget shortages provided a driving force. The UHM library system is at physical capacity. Yet there are no contingencies for further growth. Mochida observes that there is no room for remote storage. "If I had asked for an offsite storage facility from the state legislature, they would have laughed," she says. "They think that libraries are all electronic" (Mochida 2012). For the time being, space will be found through rigorous weeding and de-duplication, especially among the Asia Collection, with its overlapping holdings on Hamilton's second floor. The organizational plan put forth by Mochida's administration focused on centralization. Intermediate management would be eliminated and departments consolidated into larger units under a higher level administrator to enable greater flexibility in meeting challenges. "I wanted to create more time and resources out of what we had for the future," Mochida says. There was no lack of time spent in consultation. The library staff considered the plan over the course of three years, through retreats, drafts, review sessions, and all the management procedures for such an undertaking. Yet the final plan met resistance in the form of negative poll results gathered by the Library faculty senate, rejection by the university senate, and warnings from unions, representing the librarians and library staff, that the proposal appeared to violate collective-bargaining agreements.

Bazzell observes that the centers for Asian studies objected to having to consult with non–subject matter experts under the new plan, and the Asian librarians agreed that their relationships and tasks were not interchangeable as the plan implied (Bazzell 2012). Sinclair notes that while the plan responded to staff input, successive drafts for recombining departments seemed disconnected, as though change was being sought for its own sake, and the staff lost confidence (Sinclair 2012). Chantiny observes, "The plan had some good elements and others not so good. There was a lot of discussion, and I suppose that it demonstrated the good and bad parts of [library] faculty status" (Chantiny 2012).

Many survey responses from the librarians called for a connection between "form and function" in reorganization. There appears to have been a disconnect between staff expectations for practical change and tangible improvements, on the one hand, and an administrative vision that grappled with the future, on the other. The library is now embarking on another organizational effort from the bottom up, and in this form, the reorganization plan may have an influence on future policy after all. The dialogue continues.

As UHM grapples to find the correct structure for its outstanding services, it is clear that place—as both a concept and a reality—will remain a significant factor in its future. Indeed, in the themes of globalization that universities and libraries are embracing, UHM would be very hard to surpass as a leader in the field.

◼◼

University of Illinois
at Urbana-Champaign

The University of Illinois at Urbana-Champaign returns us to the beginning of modern librarianship in the United States. The school was chartered with the original Morrill Act of 1862 and established on what was then the frontier. It languished for the first two decades of its existence, and even in the 1880s was described as a raw environment. Rich farmland though it was, the area endured freezing temperatures in winter, and in summer, its swampy environment bred clouds of mosquitoes (Solberg 2000, 38). Change arrived with the appointment of Andrew Sloan Draper as university president in 1894. An educator from New York, Draper was animated by the same visionary impulses as Melvil Dewey to develop education as a force for improving society. In a somewhat heavy-handed and authoritarian way, Draper recruited faculty and organized the university.

Draper was succeeded in 1904 by President Edmund Janes James, who continued his mission. James's vision for the university was driven by his great admiration for the German university model, which he had experienced firsthand while earning a PhD at the University of Heidelberg. First-class research required a first-class collection, and James tied the growth of the university to that of its library (see the definitive account of the Illinois library, Solberg 2004). He was able to build on the services of Katharine Sharp, the University Librarian who had been recruited by Draper. Sharp was one of Melvil Dewey's disciples from his library school in New York, and Dewey described her as the finest female librarian in America. Sharp emulated Dewey with a ferocious work ethic with which she pursued many of Dewey's innovations. Sharp improved the reference service at Illinois, bought more relevant and interesting books, and organized the collection. She did not, however, contribute significantly to the enormous and famous collection that the library was to acquire. Her achievement, in line with her model, Dewey, was to achieve a new level of standardization and professionalism (Solberg 2000, 41). Yet her own industry proved to be her undoing. Working beyond her "natural strength," she required long periods of rest in order to function, and she took these vacations up at Dewey's club in Lake Placid, New York. She was both pushed by her need to convalesce and pulled by her devotion to Dewey. For both of these reasons, she finally resigned her position at Illinois to take up residence at Dewey's club. She remained steadfastly loyal to Dewey during the scandal that surrounded him for his familiar behavior with women. Within a short time, she suffered an untimely death when the touring car in which she was traveling around Lake Placid fell over a cliff. President James mourned the loss of his exceptional librarian.

After an exhaustive search for a successor, James settled on Phineas Windsor, with whom he was to lead the Illinois library to distinction. Far from being indifferent to the library, as university administrators are sometimes perceived to be today, James involved himself deeply in its affairs, even to the point of chiding Windsor frequently by memo over minor details. James personally oversaw the acquisition of large libraries of scholars from his beloved German universities. In 1914, he set the then unheard-of goal of collecting one million volumes. This was achieved by 1935, ten years after James's death. Illinois has remained internationally known for its collection size ever since.

The facilities that would house Illinois's famous collection also moved forward under James. Altgeld Hall, the university's first library, had been opened in 1897 under Draper's presidency. Dewey himself spoke at its inauguration ceremony. A monumental structure, Altgeld was constructed out of pink sandstone and has a vast tower anchoring one corner of its impressive façade (fig. 14). The building remains in use as the site of the mathematics department (as well as a departmental library in mathematics), and its soaring tower now houses chimes that sound daily across the campus. But within twenty years, the Illinois library had outgrown even this structure, and plans were laid for a facility that, like Altgeld, would eventually be entered on the National Registry of Historic Places and become a model for other libraries. While housing many departmental libraries in its main building, the library continued to expand into a total of over forty units, many located at satellites throughout the campus. Beyond its massive collection, Illinois has striven to become a leader in services to its campus. While this has a contemporary sound, the origins precede the recent explosion of information technology. In the late 1970s, University Librarian Hugh Atkinson, in a quest for efficiency with

Fig. 14. Altgeld Hall, the original library at the University of Illinois, now houses the mathematics department with a departmental library.

his enormous collection, inaugurated one of the first systems of library automation. Paula Kaufman, until 2013 dean of libraries and university librarian at Illinois, adds, "I could argue that Illinois was always out front in terms of its services. It is a very Midwestern place. It's never done a lot of boasting about itself" (Kaufman 2012). With its recently acquired thirteen millionth volume, Illinois remains at the forefront of academic libraries in the size and quality of its famous collection as well as its depth of technological innovation and powerful service ethic.

Transformers

The preeminence of Illinois, with its traditional division into departmental libraries, makes it an instructive subject of study at a period of change. As Kaufman observes, "Our huge collection was a treasured asset. Now, much of it is a liability" (Kaufman 2010, 8). The ease of access offered by electronic resources has increased expectations that print resources cannot meet; meanwhile, print resources still require massive funds for their maintenance. The extensively subdivided departmental libraries have also begun to show their age. Despite (or because of) its great assets, one might describe the challenge facing Illinois as double that of UCM. In addition to forging new services and resources, Illinois must work within the restrictions of its storied past. Like Transformers, the sentient machines of movie and cartoon, Illinois must seamlessly convert its parts into a new configuration. As a first step, the library has drawn down its number of departmental libraries from forty to approximately thirty. Ten of these reside in the Main Library, with the remainder located at different points around campus and in the residence hall. The Main Library and the adjacent Undergraduate Library (UGL) to which it is connected retain their historic place as the center of library operations and will be the focus of this study.

The data is relatively static for the last five years (table 5) and as such improves upon the general trend of declining library usage throughout the profession. The exception is in the significant drop in reference-related numbers. According to JoAnn Jacoby, head of Reference, Research, and Scholarly Services, the reasons for the decrease are threefold: more stringent criteria for what constitutes a reference transaction, reducing the inflated statistics of earlier periods; an actual decline in reference statistics over a ten-year period; and a slowness by some units to adopt chat reference, an area where significant growth has taken place.

Undergraduate Library

The architecture of the UGL, which was completed in 1969, flies in the face of the historical tradition of representing power and the related trend of monumentalism in library buildings; it is completely underground. One enters through one of two small structures aboveground, which enclose stairwells, and proceeds down one flight to the first of the library's two underground floors. This design apparently ensures that the library does not cast a shadow on the Morrow Plots, an adjoining field for agricultural experiment that goes back to the university's origins. Another reason for submerging the library was to preserve the open space of the campus's historic quad. Nevertheless, its innovative "light well," according to Scott Bennett, is so effective that patrons do not even realize they are underground (Bennett 2012). This well, which is two stories deep, is essentially an open courtyard surrounded by glassed-in user space. Looking up from below, patrons get the same sense of suspension in space, unusual angles, and abundant natural lighting that characterize the most modern library buildings.

The origin of an undergraduate library has been traced all the way back to 1608 at Oxford and then to 1765, when Harvard set aside "a smaller library for the common use of the college." James Canfield, librarian at Columbia, is credited with the first official undergraduate library in 1907, though it is Harvard's Lamont Library (1949) that is considered the immediate ancestor of today's institutions (Hamlin 1981, 140–141). Lori Mestre, head of the Undergraduate Library at Illinois, notes another

Table 5. Vital Statistics, University Library, Illinois, 2009–2010

Collection	13,158,748
(1.8% to 9.4% change in last 5 years)	
Circulation	1,036,873
(1.2% to 28% change in last 5 years)	
ILL:	
Lending	88,073
(–5% and 18% change in last 5 years)	
Borrowing	79,92
(–8% to 0% change in last 5 years)	
Shelf space occupied	~70%
Reference transactions	88,746
(–16% and –32% change in last 5 years)	
Instruction to groups	1,387
(–18% to 40% change in last 5 years)	
Staff	508
(–7.5% to 16% change in last 5 years)	
Budget	$40,577,401
(–5% to 16% change in last 2 years)	

Source: Official ARL Statistics (Kyrillidou and Bland 2008, 2009; Kyrillidou and Morris 2011; Kyrillidou, Morris, and Roebuck 2011; Kyrillidou and Young 2008).

Note: Parentheses indicate the highest and lowest rates of annual change in the years indicated, not necessarily in order.

flurry of development in the 1960s, a period of active library development and lavish funding (Mestre 2012). When asked to define the distinction between the UGL and the enormous Main Library building that looms over it, Mestre describes the dual functions of previous undergraduate libraries of accessibility and scholarship. These are evident in the print collection, the traditional basis of libraries, which is selected for basic introductory texts, broad coverage, and recreation. Harlequin Romances are very popular, as is other contemporary fiction. After extensive weeding made possible by the construction of an off-campus storage facility, the collection now consists of about 160,000 volumes.

"So Five Minutes Ago . . ."

Naturally, an institution so focused on accessibility has grappled with the Learning Commons concept that is so prominent in library design. Upon arrival in 2005, Mestre initiated a major overhaul of the physical space that was funded largely through donations and assistance from the university's Division of Intercollegiate Athletics (DIA). This unit, according to Kaufman, undertook a major campaign to raise $500,000 over five years and then another $500,000 over the next five years. A number of strategies were employed, including the sale of rubber wristbands and of a series of bookmarks with a picture of the library on one side and a basketball player on the other. The largest source of revenue came from leasing seat cushions and backs for bleacher seats. "We have been very fortunate for the acknowledgment by the DIA of the importance of libraries to their students," says Mestre.

The UGL undertook an inversion of its physical structure when it shifted the print collection from the top floor (repurposed for collaboration) to the bottom floor (now for quiet study), which it shares with the DVD/media collection of videos, audio books, music media, the gaming collection, and more. Seating and study areas were moved from the bottom to the top floor and renovated. This was the result of space use studies that revealed a trend toward collaborative rather than individual studying. The staple replacement furniture is a kind of tri-carrel with short partitions, not unlike those that have proven so popular at the University of Hawai'i's Student Success Center; like there, each individual carrel is equipped with a power source. The entire south wall of the upper level of the UGL features a row of group study rooms each equipped with a table, chairs, media-viewing equipment, a whiteboard, and a large-screen monitor. In addition, there are pods of sofas and the ever-popular comfy chairs. Outside the doors of the entrance to the UGL on its first floor below ground is a thriving café with a seating area that is generally occupied at all hours of the day. The library also houses other campus units, including a writer's workshop and computer lab, as well as scheduled hours for career services, the study abroad program, and advising.

"We've always had these connections, but have worked to make them more formalized within the UGL," says Mestre. A 2007 annual report of the UGL prepared by Mestre's predecessor, Lisa Janicke Hinchliffe, states that the goal is continuous improvement "to evolve the learning commons model beyond mere co-location of library and technology resources as is common at many campuses to more programmatic and service initiatives and integrations that capitalize on co-location and partnerships to create outreach and engagement opportunities" (Hinchliffe 2007, 5). Mestre adds, "We are getting away from a Learning Commons as a place and thinking of it as an integration of all the services we have, both physical and virtual" (Mestre 2012). Plans are under way for a Media Commons (not unlike the one in UHM's Student Success Center) in cooperation with the campus computing unit, CITES (Campus Information Technologies and Educational Services). The UGL's Media Commons is both a place and a service, according to Mestre. It seeks to address the curricular emphasis on group and collaborative learning as well as multimodal projects that require increasingly sophisticated technologies, such as video production with editing features. The Media Commons is being developed on the top floor and will include media technology and consulting advice for using it. The plan calls for "zones" of technology services, including an iPad gallery, a "sandbox," collaborative computing, consulting, gaming, media literacy, and a production studio.

One zone supervised by Jim Hahn, Orientation Services and Environments Librarian, prototypes mobile apps. The program, which began with mobile access to the UGL, has grown beyond technical support to incorporate the entire developmental life cycle of the technology. Focus groups determine which mobile apps students would find most useful. Hahn has trained student staff to develop these programs in-house. The apps are then tested again by more focus groups so that their assessment is built into their development. Currently, the most popular apps are for finding the location of items in the collection, which are indicated on a GPS-type display. Hahn hopes in future that this service will not only provide programs for download but will also offer consulting for the full spectrum of student patrons, from those who are relatively unfamiliar with mobile technologies to those requiring sophisticated technical advice.

Another projected zone of the Media Commons will support gaming. Library conferences and literature are full of references to games and their application to librarianship, but Illinois is one of the few institutions that has put these ideas into practice. David Ward, Reference Services Librarian at the UGL, supervises this program and has been recognized with a Presidential Citation for Gaming from the ALA. He aims to make the collection, which includes role-playing and other interactive games, as comprehensive as possible. Regarding the additional burden on collection resources, he notes, "We've had a media collection forever, and it's the same issue of trying to keep up with DVDs or books. It's all content, and it's a question of what choices we make" (Ward 2012).

A number of services spring from the collection. The recreational purpose of the UGL is clearly evident. Gaming nights allow gamers to gather together to practice their skills and learn new games or take a break from studying. Ward also provides a career service by arranging events for students to meet representatives of the gaming industry to gather information and make contacts. The collection also serves the scholarly purpose of the library as source of study for academic disciplines. The heaviest academic use of the games appears to come from the communications department, where the games are used as artifacts of cultural study that reveal values and ideology. Media studies and the Graduate School of Library and Information Science School are also heavy users. With its innovative spaces and services, the Media Commons may be making the basic Learning Commons obsolete before many libraries have put it into practice.

The UGL also offers library instruction to their traditional audience of students of introductory writing courses. Yet the content, according to Susan Avery, Instructional Services Librarian, has expanded beyond the basic library instruction model focused on the traditional written paper to address student work in multimedia and student writing in different scholarly discourses (Avery 2012). There is also new demand for instruction from ESL courses as part of the university's strategic plan for global involvement. Richard Wheeler, Visiting Associate Vice President for Academic Affairs, observes, "What we thought of as national issues twenty or thirty years ago are global issues now. And our students increasingly are going to be going into a world where some sort of knowledge of how the rest of the world lives is going to be important." Illinois already has a large international presence. "The last time I looked at the numbers, the only campus that has more international students than us is USC," Wheeler notes. (Approximately 20 percent of the Illinois student body, or 8,500 students, is international; see www.dmi.illinois.edu/cp/.) The UGL uses graduate assistants (GAs) to handle the bulk of the instruction. The GAs complete a training program that includes observation of experienced teachers, team teaching, and then individual instruction. While the focus remains on one-shot classes in person, the program supplements the in-class instruction with online LibGuides as well as a video tour and YouTube videos, one of which features a rap introduction to the UGL and its services created by a team of UGL graduate assistants. In addition, the UGL supplies library information in both print and electronic form for course texts and manuals for first-year writing classes.

Embedded

In order to reach out further to its patrons, Illinois operates a number of programs that embed librarians in their department areas, about which more will be said at a later point. Meanwhile, let's look at a variation on this approach, in which librarians are embedded in residence halls. As noted earlier, this idea has been widely touted of late as a means to enhance reference service. The Illinois program, however, goes back much further, even before the creation of the UGL, to 1948, according to Gretchen Madsen, Residence Hall Librarian (Madsen 2012). The original program was designed to serve female students, who were not allowed outside their dormitories—and hence denied access to the libraries—after dark. In its current iteration, the residence library program looks toward the future. There are currently seven residence hall libraries that operate as a mini-library network of their own. The main one is located in the Student Dining and Residential Programs building. This massive new facility, occupying two floors, houses food outlets, cafés, convenience stores, and the largest dining hall in the country outside of military bases. The residence hall library, located on the second floor next to a large lounge, comprises a room filled with the print collection and an adjacent group study room with a table, chairs, and a large-screen monitor.

The purpose of these embedded libraries is tied to the basic educational paradigm underlying the residence halls: the learning community. This concept presumes that students learn better within a stable group of people. While students can move out anytime, some choose to remain for their entire college careers. Location within such a community allows the library to address the totality of the students' experiences in a way that a traditional library cannot. For the most part, the library's functions are weighted toward recreation. Much of the print collection is devoted to popular magazines and recent fiction. The ubiquitous Harlequin Romances are extremely popular, and the best-selling novel *Fifty Shades of Grey*, with its lurid themes of bondage and other types of sexual experimentation, can hardly be kept on the shelves, according to Madsen. This last item, believe it or not, does relate to other educational programming among the residence halls. Unit One at Allen Hall has a long-standing program of inviting guests-in-residence to live and interact with its students for a week. In January 2012, Unit One hosted Tristan Taormino, sex educator, author, columnist, and adult film actress and director. She was the most prominent of a number of speakers providing "sex-positive" programming. Asked if parents objected to such material, Madsen replied that the staff use such occasions to explain that the residence halls seek to support students in every aspect of their lives without discrimination. The residence hall libraries also participate in mail delivery of books throughout campus, and the demand for their collections makes them net lenders.

The libraries do not have traditional services of reference and instruction. In part, this is because the programs are funded by the residence halls themselves, which lack sufficient funds. But the campus, Madsen observes, is already "overprogrammed." As in other spheres of activity, the library finds itself in heavy competition for its clientele. Having occupied her position for two years, Madsen is still learning about the environment and exploring opportunities for programming. She lives in the residence halls as a member of the staff and has found it useful to participate in programming outside of her library responsibilities. This allows her to interact with a wider range of students and provides visibility for the library as she discovers ways to design useful activities.

But students also retain certain traditional demands. In the sprawling residence hall environment of the main building, with its large, multi-purpose areas, quiet study areas are not easy to find. Students value the lounge outside of the library for this purpose and guard it jealously. Madsen reports that she herself has been shushed by students and reminded that she is in a library on occasions when she was speaking to her staff. Thus the residence hall libraries retain continuity with their institutional history even as the reading matter, at the least, has moved beyond the time when female students were confined indoors at night.

Main Library

The Main Library building next to the UGL is a gateway to library history. Though constructed in 1926, its design resembles common designs from the end of the previous century. Passing two oversize nude sculptures of the Daughters of Pyrrha by Lorado Taft, 1879 university alumnus, the visitor enters beneath a monumental brick façade (fig. 15). Inside, the visitor passes through the spacious Marshall Gallery and then turns right or left to ascend two flights of stairs and emerge into a large room hung with an immense chandelier and decorated in dark wood panels. A large information desk sits in the middle of the room with the circulation desk directly behind, similar to public library buildings of the nineteenth century. Consistent with that plan, wings stretch to the right and left, housing departmental libraries, while the bulk of the collection extends behind the circulation desk in the east and west stacks. The building seems to have been designed as the culmination of the architectural trends of its time, beginning with the original building and ending in the creation of the west stacks, an enormous brick cube filled almost solid with books thanks to its compact shelving. This evolution, according to Bennett, is

Fig. 15. Front
(east) entrance to
the Main Library
at Illinois.

the story of books pushing out people prior to the rise of information technology and what he describes as a third epoch of library building designed around learner-centered spaces (Bennett 2012).

A certain amount of preliminary work, however, has been done to renovate the building. An architectural study of 2006 identified needs for modernization and offered suggestions to address them (Shepley 2006). Two that have been followed include, first, improving the relationship and access between the Main Library and the UGL. While the distance is not great, the UGL's aboveground presence of two enclosed stairways, reminiscent of blockhouses, does not make for an inviting destination— during the freezing Illinois winters even less so. In fact it was because of the weather that an underground tunnel was constructed between the two buildings. The tunnel's original interior was spartan, with a number of vending machines and tiny tables and chairs bolted to the wall. But as at UC Davis, the library has gained from the attention of an undergraduate architecture class which has renovated the tunnel with pastel colors and multipurpose seating areas to make it more inviting. The university has also followed through on a recommendation to open the space of the Main Library and make it more inviting. This has been done on the Main Library's second floor with tables for computers and a lounge space. Banks of catalog cards have been removed. The circulation desk, once a forbidding rampart, has been breached with a large entrance, accessible now to undergraduates as well as graduates and faculty and leading directly into the stacks.

A radical master plan has also been developed that will transform the physical space of the library as well as its function as significantly as has ever been done. Orienting itself toward a streamlined future focused on service as opposed to collection, the library will transfer the entire UGL to the cavernous stack space in the Main Library behind its circulation desk (about which more below). The contents of the stacks will be moved to the Oak Street storage facility or to a smaller storage "box" next to the Main Library (perhaps with an automated retrieval system). The space currently occupied by the UGL will be used for special collections, which will come into more prominence as the library uses shared repositories for its other holdings. Work is going forward with the sealing of the Main Library against extreme weather. But with an estimated cost of $300 million, the time frame for the renovation is indeterminate. "The work will be done as money comes available," observes Kaufman. In the meantime, the Main Library is working out its future in its current space.

Legacy

Paula Kaufman was the fourteenth University Librarian at Illinois in a continuous list that includes Katharine Sharp herself (fifth librarian). During her term, Kaufman determined upon a change in direction. With the liabilities of the massive and famous print collection, the library will no longer pursue its top spot in ARL rankings for collection size. "This campus has long reveled in the ranking of three or two. I guess we're number two now by size of holding, and our last set of administrators and our current set of administrators have basically agreed that that's a silly thing to be holding on to when it's more important to manage our resources," Kaufman observes. Instead of focusing on collection size, the library will place more emphasis on quality of services, which have always been a strength of Illinois. The services must be sensitive to the new needs of users, and they must remain at the forefront of the profession. Kaufman employs the metaphor of a "fabric" for library services that enfold every aspect of the university without being limited by location (Kaufman 2007, 8). In replacing collections with services, Illinois is a paradigm of the changing profession of academic librarianship just as it has so long been a leader in collections.

The new services will rely heavily on consortia and networking. Currently, Kaufman argues, libraries are largely the same because they duplicate each other's print collections. Evidently, this is a poor return on investment in a grim budget climate. By combining resources in networks, libraries will be able to divest themselves of needless expense and focus resources on distinctive special collections (Kaufman 2007, 6). This is not unlike the vision promoted by Dan Greenstein (see chapter

6). Illinois's special collections already have a tradition in the acquisitions of President James from German universities and retain international distinction today.

To undertake this plan, Illinois, notwithstanding its enormous historical commitments and the depressed economy, is in remarkably good shape. The vast collection, while pressed for space, has plans for accommodation. These include the recent construction of the high-density storage Oak Street facility, about which more will be said. Weeding has been "slow and careful . . . and there are plans to weed even Oak Street of duplicate serials." The library is also doing reasonably well with its finances. "When I arrived in 2002, we had a deficit, but ever since the library has been solvent. The library has managed its money well" (Kaufman 2012). Economic change has required some change in financial strategy. As with the UC system and other state libraries, Illinois's portion of state funding has decreased, and this extra burden has been taken up largely by fundraising, with donors under the direction of the library's advancement officer. Here the library is doing better than ever, surpassing its previous goal of $45 million with $50 million in its latest fundraising effort, and ideas abound for future advancement. "The name of this building is 'Library' . . . We don't have any names; it's a naming opportunity," notes Kaufman. "For $100 million, you can have either this building [or the UGL]."

The End of the Print Storehouse . . . ?

To deal with the demands of the print collection, a major tool has been the Oak Street storage facility, opened in 2007. Some librarians see the end of huge buildings dedicated to storing books; it does, for example, appear that the rows of compact shelving in the west stacks have reached the limit in density. But the Oak Street facility surpasses even this, with its high-density storage achieved through new technologies, according to Tom Teper, Associate University Librarian for Collections and Technical Services. Materials at Oak Street are organized by size rather than call number. Volumes are set in trays that are raised up to forty feet and set back at some depth. Currently, an attendant in a lift retrieves items, but technology for remote retrieval could create new efficiencies in future modules on campus. In the newest module, these gigantic stacks are placed on rails to enable compact shelving and approach the absolute limit of a space filled with paper. The Oak Street facility has a capacity for seven million volumes, and in addition to storage, Oak Street undertakes preservation with state-of-the-art technologies. The facility expands the library's stewardship of its print collection, and in future, it will curate other media.

With the new space available in the old stacks, the libraries have sought to make them more accessible. In addition to the construction of the large entryway, new signage has been posted inside to make navigation easier, and improved lighting has been installed. But modernization is limited by the basic architecture of the building. Its cast-iron shelving dates from the early twentieth century and, as part of the load-bearing structure, cannot be moved. The stacks retain for patrons the sensation from earlier library buildings of being suspended amidst books. The very size and complexity of the collection raises an additional obstacle since it is virtually impossible to get a precise idea of how full the shelves are. Staff speak in terms of moving "bubbles" of open space, and a figure of 75 percent is the closest any will approach to an estimate. For certain call number ranges, it is not possible for patrons to locate items without the assistance of staff. Like Moria, the fabulous underground city of dwarves in Tolkien's *Lord of the Rings* trilogy, the exquisitely organized information in the Illinois stacks retains a sense of mystery.

The confusion in the stacks results not just from its size but also from a cataloging issue that goes back in history. Under the direction of Katharine Sharp, Illinois adopted the Dewey Decimal Classification (DDC) that was the creation of her idol. When other academic libraries changed to the Library of Congress system in the 1970s, Illinois, perhaps because of its pre-eminence or the mere size of its collection, chose not to, instead relying upon a locally modified version of the DDC. When it finally adopted the new system, it was too late to make a full conversion, so Illinois labors under two different call number systems. This is an enormous problem that is also completely intractable; there are simply not enough resources for a complete conversion. The library has settled for targeted conversions of particular departments. But there is no plan for complete or even retrospective conversion for collections that have switched over. This reliance upon a locally modified DDC, says Teper, historically prevented Illinois from taking advantage of shelf-ready services that do not support Dewey collections.

Illinois is also grappling with a familiar set of issues for their technical services that maintain the collections, through a unit called Content Access Management. Michael Norman, department head, describes initiatives to reduce cataloging backlogs with SWAT teams of graduate assistants (Norman 2012). Catalogers themselves are developing "good enough" policies to expedite their work. A reorganization of non-Roman cataloging is under way. And new connections are being explored between cataloging and acquisition to speed up processing. As with UCD and to a certain extent UHM, technical processing is moving upstream into acquisitions, with cataloging done there when possible. Given the extent of the collection, there are limits to cross-training cataloging staff between different formats to streamline their work, but the department aims to increase the number of cataloging records submitted to OCLC. Not only will Illinois be providing a service to the profession, but, this time the size of its collection works to advantage: the library can achieve a considerable amount of savings in credits for these records. As at UCD, the cataloging department is also exploring metadata services. Currently, its focus is on converting MARC records by machine into an XML format so that their metadata can be mined more efficiently by search tools. Finally, the library, according to Teper, is exploring patron-driven demand. In one system, a record is placed in the catalog, and when an order is placed for document delivery, the item is purchased and rushed to the library. But patron-driven demand is envisioned as a complement to and not a replacement for the work of selectors.

Technology Planning

The second of Illinois's three Associate University Librarians, Beth Sandore Namachchivaya, supervises the Office of Information Technology Policy and Planning. This is defined to include the traditional systems department. But Sandore has also worked outside the library on a campuswide task force on cyberinfrastructure. The task force has made an integrated attempt with campus partners such as CITES to develop coherent data management practices for the entire campus. It was found that individual campus entities have acquired gigantic storage capacities known only to themselves that need to be coordinated (Sandore 2012). "One of our high-level realizations that we wanted to make the campus sensitive to is that storage is the new network of thirty years ago. . . . Storage is part of the application that we use, the stuff we produce from it. . . . It's much more a part of our infrastructure than we ever thought before. So, it can't be viewed in a modular way. It has to be looked at in an integrated way. That is really, bottom line, what we discovered" (Sandore 2012). Where the library will invest its expertise and where it will outsource tasks in cyberinfrastructure remains to be seen. Sandore's portfolio also includes support for library faculty research. As faculty, Illinois librarians have heavy requirements for research and publication. To assist

them—and in the process fund much of the library's innovative research—Sandore is working on a mentoring program for grant writing
that pairs experienced grant writers with newcomers. The third element
of her portfolio, Research Services, blends into User Services, the province of Illinois's third Associate University Librarian, Susan Searing.

New Service Models

The charge of centralizing Illinois's vast departmental structure falls most
directly on User Services. The response has taken the form of a just-
completed three-year program of New Service Models (NSMs) under
the leadership of JoAnn Jacoby, who served as coordinator of the NSM
programs from 2008 to 2011. During this period of time, Illinois has
both designed and implemented approximately twenty major reorganiza-
tional initiatives. Three features stand out from this panorama: (1) the
awesome organizational complexity of the program as a whole; (2) the
highly articulated nature of the developmental process; the records of the
NSMs show an awareness of how much work to take on, who to consult,
how often to review, and when to change direction; and (3) a capacity for
following through on initiatives. Many ideas first imagined at the program's outset such a short time ago present themselves as new, attractively
furnished facilities ready for business.

Just as the choice of database options is basic to the field of information literacy, the selection of elements for library reorganization could be
said to constitute a form of "management literacy." Discarding the older
paradigms of top-down or bottom-up, the NSMs offer a different organizational vision altogether. The building block of this reorganization is
called a "hub." This may be described as a node of activity spanning both
the virtual and real and past and present in preserving Illinois's standards
of excellence while adding something new. "We like the term, 'hubs,'" notes
Searing. Approximately sixty proposals were solicited from the library
staff for review by the library executive committee. Kaufman attributes
part of the program's success to this phase: "I have a very thoughtful executive committee." She adds that the committee's elected nature, mandated
by university bylaws, enables full transparency. This committee supplied
some of its own proposals, and Jacoby describes efforts to mesh the administrative and staff levels of vision as an essential part of her work and
a key to the success of the NSM program (Jacoby 2012). Kaufman adds
that she undertook meetings at least once a semester with campus deans
and administration to see which initiatives might have broader support.

With the projects selected, they were then put through a two-part program of development and implementation with iterated reviews. To prepare, Jacoby took a course in project management at Illinois's Graduate School of Library and Information Science (GSLIS), founded by Katharine Sharp and consistently ranked as the top graduate library school in the nation. Searing adds that Illinois's particular model evolved over time (Searing 2012). One of the goals of the three-year project was not just the reorganizations themselves but the development of a management model that would sustain the library's evolution. The administration now has the confidence to proceed with future reorganizations and to make the right decisions in a complex, highly distributed organization.

Notwithstanding the rapid progress of the NSMs, they did not overcome the major issues facing librarianship without conflict. "I don't want you to think that everything was a bed of roses; some of the discussions were very difficult," observes Kaufman. A pillar of the management model was extensive consultation with campus stakeholders. Faculty were recruited for both development and implementation teams to express their viewpoints. Numerous town hall meetings were also held, where participants were not shy about venting their objections to change. "I just listened, and I didn't respond very much. Occasionally I did when people would say outrageous things," Kaufman observes in a distillation of the measured, responsive spirit that pervades the NSMs. Resistance to change also appeared among library staff, and retirements played a role in some cases. But within the management model that evolved, these conversations resulted in change. A full review of the NSMs would require far more space than available here, so representative examples will be discussed instead.

Reference

Reference for both the Main Library and the UGL consists of one Main/UGL hub. The hub comprises a large circular information desk on the second floor of the Main Library, a reference point in the UGL, and a virtual reference desk (currently located in the UGL) where staff conduct chat reference. The in-person reference desk at the UGL has been reduced to a small table that will soon be phased out in favor of roving staff with iPads. The hub is designed to bring together staff from all units in the Main and Undergraduate Libraries and deploy them to the most active service points. The virtual reference desk, which is seeing a rapid increase in usage, has been especially busy.

The enormous Reference Reading Room on the second floor of the Main Library, which was filled with an extensive collection of print reference materials, has undergone radical weeding, and the original reading room tables have been cleared of the tabletop shelves to create more user space. A noncirculating collection of retrospective reference materials was created near the entrance of the main stacks to house encyclopedias, bibliographies, and yearbooks, which although dated, are of enduring reference value and more easily used when all volumes are available.

The new reference model pools staff from the departmental libraries who may be assigned to both the virtual and Main Library desks along with graduate student assistants. The basic theme is one of extreme consolidation. However, Jacoby, looking ahead, has another vision of what reference might look like. Describing a study of hospital care, she explains that the quality of service was not correlated to the wealth of the hospital but to the coordination among its doctors. Patients who were seen by specialists working independently had high costs and poor outcomes, whereas those cared for by a cohesive team of doctors did much better. Is it possible, Jacoby wonders, that the same might be true for reference, so that teams of subject specialist librarians and technologists could be assembled around particular research questions and individual scholarly needs? The removal of departmental barriers may enable some new level of cooperation among reference teams.

SSHEL

The creation of the Social Sciences, Health, and Education Library (SSHEL) is an example of a centralized NSM. Three former libraries, the Business and Economics Library, the Education and Social Science Library, and the Applied Health Sciences Library, were combined into one. The odd man of the group here was the Applied Health Sciences Library, but its reconception was a major driver behind the project. The Applied Health Sciences Library served its own college of the same name. The library possessed a deep collection with unusual but fascinating pieces, such as *Championship Fighting: Explosive Punching and Aggressive Defense* (1950), a lengthy and detailed tome on the technique of boxing by heavyweight champion Jack Dempsey. With such items, the Applied Health Sciences Library posted exceptionally high rates of circulation and was closely identified with its academic unit. However, its disciplinary bounds intersected with the changing and rapidly expanding field of health, which included interdisciplinary initiatives in wellness. Moreover, many of the methods and resources overlapped with social sciences. It was decided that the best way to meet these needs was SSHEL, serving to tie together its component libraries. Even now, SSHEL, which is still undergoing renovation, retains something of a divided identity, with half of the library on the north side of the first floor and half of the library on the south side, bracketing the open area inside the entrance. Both areas will offer workstations and lounge areas for use along with their collections.

There was significant resistance to change both inside and out, according to Nancy O'Brien, head of SSHEL. She observes, "The children's and young adult literature collection is one of the highest used collections in the library's system based on circulation data and it's probably because it's a very active program" (O'Brien 2012). Such a resource inspired protectiveness from its librarians. External to the library, much of the resistance to the reorganization came from the Applied Health Sciences faculty, who sought to safeguard their popular library with its distinct identity. Associate Dean of GSLIS Linda Smith, who was involved on the planning committee, notes that an administrator for Applied Health Sciences proved critical. "The associate dean . . . is a very thoughtful, reasonable individual . . . Being an administrator, he realized that resources are finite, and he explored how to work with the library to get the best support for the unit" (L. Smith 2012). O'Brien echoes this point. "There was a feeling that the change was coming so we adapted to it" (O'Brien 2012). Cross-training of the librarians into new areas of expertise is a huge issue, and it will be addressed with an extensive program. The library is also coming to grips with the Main/UGL reference hub. Under the new plan, librarians are supposed to staff the hub, not their own subject library. But this raises the possibility of patrons getting referred by SSHEL to the main information desk for the initial contact and then back down to their starting point for a subject specialist. SSHEL is considering an intermediate service point to forestall these situations.

Embedded Again

In some cases, combining departmental libraries or even maintaining them was not feasible, so it was decided to close them and embed librarians into their academic units. With the libraries' print materials distributed to other locations, the librarians work part-time at their academic units while also managing a virtual library portal to disciplinary information (Searing 2012). This model has been applied to libraries for the School of

Labor and Employment Relations, the College of Business, and, perhaps, most intriguingly, GSLIS.

Terry Weech, as a faculty member at GSLIS, provides a user's perspective on the embedded model. Describing the entire reorganization plan, he explains, "In the first two years, there were lots of rough spots . . . but things are running a lot smoother now. To some extent, it seems to be how long you can weather it, but staff worked hard to smooth the transition for the users." For the new embedded model, he notes, "I always considered [the Library and Information Science Library] to be a central part of what a great university library would have that respects the research of librarians. . . . But it's worked pretty well in large part because of the access to electronic information that really has helped the transition considerably." He continues, "I mean I certainly do miss the social aspect of it. I miss a place to go where I would see students and colleagues working. But I must admit the last year or two when it was still in existence, I would go over there and there would hardly be anybody there because they were all using their own computers" (Weech 2012). This response is consistent with the varied but generally positive results of assessment studies conducted by Searing, the embedded GSLIS librarian, during the transition (Searing and Greenlee 2011; Searing 2009).

Humanities

Another consolidation in the same spirit as SSHEL is the combination of the modern languages and English libraries into a Literatures and Languages Library. This occupies a new space at one end of what used to be the Reference Reading Room. The Literatures and Languages Library itself may be something of a transition state: pending the removal of technical services from the second floor, a huge U-shaped footprint, currently divided by walls, is being considered for a center for humanities librarianship. The reorganization of the humanities libraries touches on some deep issues. While traditionally the heaviest users of libraries and the very essence of the text-heavy departmental libraries that formed the core of the German university, humanities have found their position steadily eroded in libraries since World War II. As observed earlier, the development of technology in that conflict, especially having to do with computers and automation, was seized on by scientists to reorganize libraries. The humanities have never really caught on to the Information Revolution as the sciences have. Thus, as librarians move into the future, their major historical constituents are being left behind.

(For a detailed report on the usage habits and expectations of humanities scholars, see Brown et al. 2006.)

This gap was evident in the town hall meetings on library organization, according to Kaufman, where the loudest objections often came from faculty in the humanities; some claimed that she was ending "scholarship as I know it." Associate Professor of English Renée Trilling has served on both the implementation team for the Literatures and Languages Library and the campuswide faculty senate, and she describes the library reorganization as "embattled" (Trilling 2012). For the Literatures and Languages Library, she observes that the collection for English was significantly reduced (by 30–35 percent) by transfers to the main stacks (an onsite, browsable collection) and from the main stacks to the remote storage facility (request only). While her own work was largely unaffected—she receives books in her campus mailbox from a document delivery service—it has affected her colleagues. "Many of those who like to browse the collection are no longer able to do so. There's a sense that a lot of the library renovation with its lounge areas has been oriented toward students and not researchers" (Trilling 2012).

But while moving away from some features of the traditional departmental library model on the one hand, the library has offered new services on the other. Illinois is one of a number of libraries pioneering digital humanities. Harriett Green, English and Digital Humanities Librarian, describes an array of tools offered by the library for doing OCR (optical character recognition) on digitized texts, conducting data mining of texts, creating visualizations, and GIS mapping (Green 2012; the many tools for digital humanities research can be found at www.library .illinois.edu/sc/resources/resources_software). She also describes a new collection of online teaching and research products created by faculty that are beginning to play a role in their evaluation. Associate Professor of English Ted Underwood enlarges on the impact of these new tools on humanities research. Digital humanities, he observes, broadly divides into three branches: text mining, the critique of new media—such as games—and blogging, and social media (Underwood 2012). He notes that he himself was inspired to pursue this work from his original specialty of British literature by John Unsworth, former dean of GSLIS. The data mining that he has studied has already enabled new discoveries. British Romanticism, one of the major movements of literary history, was inaugurated in 1798 by William Wordsworth, who determined to break from the stylized poetry of the eighteenth century and use the plain language of everyday discourse. But by mining contemporary texts for word frequencies, Underwood has found that Wordsworth's plain and simple language was not so, and that he was calling on another body of literary discourse that already existed (Underwood and Sellers 2012). On the subject of blogging, Underwood notes that communication among colleagues takes place at a higher tempo and is more democratic. "I don't always know if I'm talking to an historian or a sociologist and it doesn't really matter." He continues, "I think we're on the cusp of a lot of changes" in terms of the way that digital humanities will affect literary scholarship (Underwood 2012).

Scholarly Commons

To facilitate its new directions, the Literatures and Languages Library is connected to yet another NSM that has a more global ambition than the consolidation of departmental libraries: the Scholarly Commons. The Scholarly Commons is an adaptation of the Learning Commons that favors advanced researchers over undergraduates. Open for two years, it has been newly moved to a large room that is still in the process of being fitted with hardware and is designed as a hub for scholarly support services as well as a work area. One of the functions of the Scholarly Commons is to help support the library's repository for university research, IDEALS, or the Illinois Digital Environment for Access to Learning and Scholarship. The major tool for this is the open source program DSpace. In addition to DSpace, Illinois uses many of the other tools, such as digital object identifiers and data management plans, used by the California Digital Library, with whom the library has cooperated.

To complement repository publication, the Scholarly Commons also offers a copyright consultancy to educate and inform users about their publication rights, although the service stops short of legal advice, according to Sarah Shreeves, co-coordinator of the Scholarly Commons (Shreeves 2012). This service is important to scholarly communication since many faculty, as Trilling notes, are concerned about how their publishing rights might be restricted by publication in a repository. This issue was echoed by Shana Brown, Associate Professor of History at UHM, who wondered about the effect of repositories on small academic presses, which are struggling financially and which she wishes to support (Brown 2012). According to Shreeves, "We get this question a lot." The response, she says, is to cast publishing as an ecosystem whose parts all depend on each other and to explain that open access to information is a desirable long-term goal for everyone.

To publicize its services, the Scholarly Commons has initiated a significant new trend in instruction. As a complement to the UGL's one-shot sessions for undergraduates, the Scholarly Commons offers a program of thirty-five different drop-in classes, called the "Savvy Researcher," for more advanced researchers on the new services and hardware offered by the commons. According to Merinda Kaye Hensley, co-coordinator of the commons, the most popular class teaches how to create publishable photos of archival materials (Hensley 2012). The software most in demand is the IBM program SPSS Statistics. The commons is also affiliated with a cluster of campuswide services to promote digital research that include the Illinois Informatics Institute (or I3) and the Institute for Computing in Humanities, Arts and Social Science (I-CHASS).

The focus of the Scholarly Commons on information technology is being paralleled by another effort at the library aimed to address one of the most significant challenges for library instruction: the migration to online learning. Wheeler provides context for Illinois. Following a failed systemwide effort in this direction, the Global Campus Initiative, the approach at Illinois has been highly decentralized, with most of the initiative in various master's programs. Meanwhile, the target of online instruction that librarians are tracking has moved, thanks to the arrival of MOOCs. "The university," notes Wheeler, "is on the second wave of getting onto the Coursera train. . . . Coursera has received a very vigorous response from our faculty. Many are offering courses and many more would like to offer courses. It's going to become more and more prominent" (Wheeler 2012). To address the total phenomenon of online instruction, Illinois librarians have not been behind in using LibGuides or participating in course management systems. But in addition to these, the library has recently acquired a license for Blackboard Collaborate (formerly Elluminate), "with an eye toward increasing online instruction" (Searing 2012). The aim, according to Searing, is to develop online workshops similar to the ones offered by the Savvy Researcher series as well as "new webinar-style offerings, tied to courses and/or promoted separately."

Searing also notes that chat reference, often seen as a quick answer service, is being reimagined as a tool for online instruction. "Our usage is much higher than peer libraries, and it's still growing. Our chat reference service is very much infused with our instructional mission, and training librarians and grad assistants for the 'virtual desk' is centered on using the teachable moment of a reference interaction to boost patrons' information literacy" (Searing 2012). The traditional reference interview that David Michalski is trying to keep from going "out the door" at UCD with the dismantling of the triage reference system appears to be coming "in at the window" at Illinois in the form of chat reference.

Reorganization is naturally tied to assessment, and Illinois has just hired an assessment coordinator for this purpose. Current plans call for her to develop a culture of assessment to amplify the current program of annual unit reports, occasional LibQUAL surveys, and a number of individual projects. In addition, now that the three-year development plan of the New Service Models has ended, Kaufman sees assessment as supplying triggers for future changes in direction.

Network

Kaufman envisions Illinois participating in a broader system for most of its collection and many of its services, and while the large picture remains to be drawn, a surprising amount of history is already in place. Illinois belongs to the Consortium of Institutional Cooperation (CIC), a group of traditional midwestern institutions whose libraries have been cooperating for fifty years, joined in 2013 by Rutgers University and the University of Maryland. The HathiTrust was one outgrowth of their work. Currently, the CIC is working on digitization with Google. Campuses within the University of Illinois system are also sharing expertise with CIC, especially when it comes to language specialists in cataloging. Another network, the Consortium of Academic Research Libraries in Illinois (CARLI), includes Illinois along with eighty other libraries in its tightly integrated ILL program. As Illinois moves into the twenty-first century, it is poised to continue its illustrious history through its strong service ethic and its great depth of organizational and technical innovation.

Conclusion

■■

"That was taken out of context . . ."
Generic statement in popular media

One purpose of this study is to supply the ever-elusive "context" to the future of academic libraries. And one way to do that is to view the multifarious issues of the profession from the perspective of the single library—a campus-scale metric. How does the individual library make sense of all the competing demands on its attention and resources? This approach has the benefit of providing a conceptual framework for processing issues as well as practical outcomes since, sooner rather than later, individual libraries will need to begin turning questions into policies and budgets. The sevenfold scheme outlined in the historical review and carried through in our case studies provides one way to accomplish all this. No library is advancing with equal speed on all fronts, so the seven headings can be applied to see where a library is directing its energies and to what effect.

But a second outcome emerges. While it is possible to apply the seven areas as a strict set of rubrics, this would be unnatural and would miss a lot of information. Nor are the various categories perfectly distinct; they typically combine with each other in patterns that are highly complex. What emerges is a unique profile for each campus that reveals the management paradigm of "organization as organism": UCD, with its scaling up of traditional services and as a node within the UC, its transcendence to the system level and beyond; UCM, with its double commitment to both a system presence and a revitalized building space; UHM, with its visionary cyber-infrastructure, outstanding area services, and cultural sensitivity; and Illinois, with its technological innovation and dazzling internal reorganization. The organism model, as opposed to the hierarchical/mechanistic model or the political/coalition model, captures the complexity of factors—material, organizational, logistical, financial, psychological, emotional, historical, and more—that go into the operation of a library, while at the same time allowing the whole to be considered as a single entity seeking its way through its environment.

Some themes emerge across the case studies that correlate with discussions in the literature. The Learning Commons in various forms is becoming the standard for building design and reference delivery. As Scott Bennett predicts, "If you want to know what the end of libraries will look like, you have a choice—not really a choice. Library space will look like common space in academic buildings; common space in academic buildings will look like libraries" (Bennett 2012). Scholarly communication in its broadest sense is playing a crucial role. This includes the collection and curation of new media and tools for disseminating it that fall outside of the traditional channels of peer-reviewed publication. System-level coordination in the form of shared repositories, collection building, and technical services also appears to be a universal movement.

These trends and more unite the case studies. But they are at least counterbalanced by the differences between the institutions. Each resides in a radically different context and has evolved unique solutions to its challenges. We can return to the question of the representative value of the four cases selected here. There are suggestive juxtapositions among them. Illinois and UCM are the extremes of the large and the small. UCD and UHM, by contrast, are relatively midsize. But UCM and UCD form a separate group as relatively integrated within the tightly cohesive UC system in contrast to the more autonomous UHM and Illinois, both of which are the flagship campuses of their states. And within their system, UCM and UCD contrast as the brand-new and the relatively traditional. Within these parameters of old, new, large, and small, as well as more or less funded and more or less networked, this set of libraries encompasses a great deal of the issues facing academic librarianship. But as one looks closer and sees endless relationships between them, one gets a sense of the complexity of libraries and begins to doubt whether there is such a thing as a truly representative set of libraries that could stand for the whole.

Our case studies also allow us to glance at larger questions of library history, but even so, it is impossible to settle on any one of the three great paradigms of radical change, hybridization, or a recycling of the same themes. There are indications of all three within the case studies. The highly successful Learning Commons at the Sinclair Library at UHM turns out to bear close similarities not just to the undergraduate library that preceded it but also to the taro patch of the School of Hawai'ian Knowledge, which anchors an ancient, indigenous system of knowledge. Nancy O'Brien, quoting from Ecclesiastes in reference to the SSHEL NSM and her career at Illinois, reminds us that "there is nothing new under the sun." One could probably say with some justification that the pace of change now is faster than heretofore, but in what direction—forward, sideways, or around in a circle—remains unknown.

It is also worth noting that the foremost innovations of our case studies have been more lateral than forward. That is, they are less about creating something radically new than a clever repurposing of what is already there. For UCD these include adaptations in medical librarianship to general library services and scaling up traditional services for an online environment. For UCM, its radical reorganization of building space and redefinition of special collections. For UHM, Tokiko Bazzell's movement outside of the traditional academic milieu to collaborate with local cultural institutions, and Karen Peacock's development of training opportunities for Pacific librarians out of what began as acquisitions trips. For Illinois, Jim Hahn's development of a prototyping program for mobile library apps that receives grants, offers new services, and provides career opportunities for students. These are a mere handful of examples among too many to name. The interstices of current library practice contain innovations more radical and creative than any speculation in the literature.

Indeed, these lateral movements as the signature of the future should come as no surprise, as the precedents are all around us. The humble sandwich, invented by an obscure English earl (otherwise known for giving his name to newly discovered islands in the Pacific), lay quiescent for centuries until it became the basis of the fast-food industry. An obscure mathematical problem solved by genius Alan Turing and used to break military codes in World War II became the basis for desktop computer technology. A communications system designed to connect research computers (ARPANET) for the Defense Department has been converted into a tool for "sexting." One gets a sense from these surprising correlations that librarians need another model of the future. For all the complex technologies discussed and the visionary futures imagined, what underlies much of library futurism is a faith in the habit of the practical librarian going from one step to the next and devising a clean-cut solution—a new killer app—to solve each problem. This is all to the good, but such a vision of the future is incomplete, as can be demonstrated by rewinding it into a theory of history. Such a future would correspond to a history that develops in a simple linear fashion, and that is evidently not how history works.

Some alternative models are worth looking at. James M. McPherson, pre-eminent historian of the American Civil War, describes that complex event in terms of a "contingent" theory of history (McPherson 1988, 858). Events unfolded because of circumstances coming together at a particular time and place in the sequence that they did—not because of fundamental determining forces. James Burke, working in the history of science, comes up with a similar conclusion: "Accident and unforeseen circumstances play

Fig. 16. The new library:
Repurposing space, accessing
knowledge.

a leading role in innovation" (Burke 1978). The future, he says, is all around us, waiting to be resynthesized and repurposed. The case studies in this book offer ample evidence for both of these models.

As far as a procedure for librarians to follow in this bewildering milieu, the organizational theories of Colonel John Boyd furnish some answers. There is no formula for an environment undergoing continual change. Instead, librarians must find the leverage points that allow them to intervene in the evolving system with maximum effect. At UHM, for example, these correspond to the disciplinary centers that integrate the work of instructional faculty with library departments. At Illinois, the leverage points are the NSMs and their hubs. Then, librarians must design a system of rapid decision cycling to process information and correct their course. At UCM, this corresponds to the team of library managers. At Illinois, decisions are made by an elected executive committee and implemented via a two-stage development and implementation process that has been tailored to the campus culture and which is subject to continual review. There are no procedures to recommend but only principles of adaptation (fig. 16).

And what of the vision and values guiding all of this? The term "symbolic librarianship" has been used by Webb to signify the special role that libraries play in the collective consciousness (Webb 2000b, 8). Librarians, in turn, are acutely aware of that role and of the expectations that come with it. Evidence abounds of the enormous energy and creativity of librarians, driven not by competition but by a service ethic. No matter what kind of fix students manage to get themselves into—trying to pull together a paper at the last minute or struggling to find the right resource—they will always find the librarian there, withholding judgment and providing help within the bounds of possibility. In a time of deep national questioning of basic social organization and values of responsibility, productivity, competition, and community, the library emerges as a unique place combining all those values. What libraries symbolize is society's best idea about itself.

Works Cited

Abbott, Bruce. 2012. Interview. University of California, Davis. April 27.

Abrams, Stephen, John Kunze, and David Loy. 2009. "An Emergent Micro-Services Approach to Digital Curation Infrastructure." Paper read at iPRES 2009: The Sixth International Conference on Preservation of Digital Objects, San Francisco.

ACRL Research Planning and Review Committee. 2010. "2010 Top Ten Trends in Academic Libraries: A Review of the Current Literature." *C&RL News* 71 (6): 286–292.

Applegate, Rachel. 2008. "Whose Decline? Which Academic Libraries Are 'Deserted' in Terms of Reference Transactions?" *Reference & User Services Quarterly* 48 (2): 176–189.

Arakawa, Melissa. 2012. Interview. University of Hawai'i at Mānoa. July 23.

Association of American Colleges and Universities. 2000. Information Literacy Competency Standards for Higher Education. Association of American Colleges and Universities. www.ala.org/acrl/standards /informationliteracycompetency.

Atlas, Michael C., Danny P. Wallace, and Connie Fleet. 2005. "Library Anxiety in the Electronic Era, or Why Won't Anybody Talk to Me Anymore?" *Reference & User Services Quarterly* 44 (4): 314–319.

Avery, Susan. 2012. Interview. University of Illinois at Urbana-Champaign. September 12.

Barclay, Donald. 2007. "Creating an Academic Library for the Twenty-First Century." *New Directions for Higher Education*, no. 139 (Fall): 103–115.

———. 2012. Interview. University of California, Merced. June 11.

Bazzell, Tokiko. 2012. Interview. University of Hawai'i at Mānoa. July 17.

Bennett, Scott. 2009. "Libraries and Learning: A History of Paradigm Change." *Portal: Libraries and the Academy* 9 (2): 181–197.

———. 2012. Interview. University of Illinois at Urbana-Champaign. September 12.

Bhavnagri, Navaz P., and Veronica Bielat. 2005. "Faculty-Librarian Collaboration to Teach Research Skills: Electronic Symbiosis." *Reference Librarian* 43 (89/90): 121–138.

Bibliographic Services Task Force. 2005. "Rethinking How We Provide Bibliographic Services for the University of California." Final Report.

http://libraries.universityofcalifornia.edu/groups/files
/bstf/docs/Final.pdf.

Blank, Phil. 2003. "Virtual Reference at Duke: An Informal History." *Reference Librarian* 38 (79/80): 215–224.

Booth, Char. 2009. *Informing Innovation: Tracking Student Interest in Emerging Library Technologies at Ohio University*. Chicago: Association of College and Research Libraries.

Bowler, Meagan, and Kori Street. 2008. "Investigating the Efficacy of Embedment: Experiments in Information Literacy Integration." *Reference Services Review* 36 (4): 438–449.

Bradley, William. 2012. "Jerry Brown Rides a Wave with National Implications." *Huffington Post*, November 20. www.huffingtonpost.com /william-bradley/jerry-brown-rides-a-wave-_b_2164331.html.

Bridges, Karl. 2004. "Boyd Cycle Theory in the Context of Non-cooperative Games: Implications for Libraries." *Library Philosophy and Practice* 6 (2). www.webpages.uidaho.edu/~mbolin/bridges2.htm.

Brown, Elizabeth W., and Gina Calia-Lotz. 2005. "Migrations in E-Publishing: A Perspective on New Roles for Librarians." In *Migrations in Society, Culture, and the Library: WESS European Conference, Paris, 2004*, edited by Tom Kilton and Ceres Birkhead. Chicago: Association of College and Research Libraries.

Brown, Shana. 2012. Interview. University of Hawai'i at Mānoa. July 26.

Brown, Stephen C., Robb Ross, David Gerrard, Mark Greengrass, and Jared Bryson. 2006. "RePAH: A User Requirements Analysis for Portals in the Arts and Humanities." Final Report. Leicester, UK: De Montfort University; Sheffield, UK: University of Sheffield.

Budd, John M. 2005. *The Changing Academic Library: Operations, Culture, and Environments*. Chicago: American Library Association.

Bundy, Alan. 2000. "Forward with Imagination: Innovative Library Client Services for the 21st Century." In *Virtual Libraries, Virtual Communities*, proceedings of the 21st annual IATUL [International Association of Technological University Libraries] conference, Queensland University of Technology, Brisbane, Queensland, Australia, July 3–7.

Burke, James. 1978. *Connections*. Boston: Little, Brown.

Burke, Liz. 2008. "Models of Reference Services in Australian Academic Libraries." *Journal of Library and Information Science* 40 (4): 269–286.

California Digital Library. 2010. "UC3 Curation Foundations." UC Curation Center (UC3). https://confluence.ucop.edu/download /attachments/13860983/UC3-Foundations-latest.pdf.

Calter, Mimi, Elliott Shore, and Christa Williford. 2010. International Digital Library Research & Development Meeting, Stanford University,

November 29–December 1, 2009. Summary Report. https://lib
.stanford.edu/files/INTL_LIB_R&D_Partic_FinalA.pdf.

Campbell, Jared. 2012. Interview. University of Illinois at Urbana-Champaign.
July 11.

Cardina, Christen, and Donald Wicks. 2004. "The Changing Roles of Academic Reference Librarians over a Ten-Year Period." *Reference & User
Services Quarterly* 44 (2): 133–141.

Carlson, Amy. 2012. Interview. University of Hawai'i at Mānoa. July 24.

Carroll, C. Edward. 1970. *The Professionalization of Education for Librarianship.*
Metuchen, NJ: Scarecrow Press.

Cayetano, Benjamin J. 2000. *Hawai'i's Emerging New Economy: A Progress
Report.* Honolulu: Hawai'i Dept. of Business, Economic Development
and Tourism, 2000.

Chantiny, Martha. 2012. Interview. University of Hawaii at Mānoa. July 20.

Chowdhury, Gobinda. 2001. "Digital Libraries and Reference Services: Present
and Future." *Journal of Documentation* 58 (3): 258–283.

Clariza, Elena Maria. 2012. Interview. University of Hawai'i at Mānoa. July 18.

Connaway, Lynn Silipigni, and Marie L. Radford. 2011. "Seeking Synchronici-
ty: Revelations and Recommendations for Virtual Reference." Dublin,
OH: OCLC Research. www.oclc.org/reports/synchronicity.en.html.

Coram, Robert. 2002. *Boyd: The Fighter Pilot Who Changed the Art of War.*
Boston: Little, Brown.

Council of University Librarians. 2010. "Next-Generation of Technical Services
Phase 2 Final Reports." December 14. http://libraries
.universityofcalifornia.edu/about/uls/ngts/docs/CoUL
_Priorities_Cover_2010.pdf.

Crawford, Walt, and Michael Gorman. 1995. *Future Libraries: Dreams, Mad-
ness & Reality.* Chicago: American Library Association, 1995.

Cruse, Patricia. 2012. University of California Curation Center (UC3). University of California, California Digital Library. Accessed July 11. www
.cdlib.org/services/uc3/.

Cummings, Joel, Lara Cummings, and Linda Frederiksen. 2007. "User Prefer-
ences in Reference Services: Virtual Reference and Academic Libraries." *Portal: Libraries and the Academy* 7 (1): 81–96.

Davidson, Sara. 2011. "Evaluating Information Literacy Skills of Writing 10
Students." University of California, Merced, Library.

———. 2012. "WRI 10 Student Portfolios: Analysis of 'Research Ethics'
Cover Letters." University of California, Merced, Library.

Davidson, Sara, and Susan Mikkelsen. 2009. "Desk Bound No More: Reference
Services at a New Research University Library." *Reference Librarian* 50
(4): 346–355.

Davis-Millis, Nina, and Thomas Owens. 1997. "Two Cultures: A Social
    History of the Distributed Library Initiative at MIT." In *Restructuring
    Academic Libraries: Organizational Development in the Wake of Techno-
    logical Change*, edited by Charles A. Schwartz. Chicago: Association of
    College and Research Libraries.
Davis, Rebecca. 2012. Interview. University of California, Davis. April 24.
Dawrs, Stu. 2010–2011. "The Archivist of Oceania." *Hana Hou! The Magazine
    of Hawaiian Airlines*, December–January. www.hanahou.com
    /pages/magazine.asp?MagazineID=50&Action=DrawArticle
    &ArticleID=932.
Dooley, Jim. 2012. Interview. University of California, Merced. June 13.
Dougherty, Richard M., and Lisa McClure. 1997. "Repositioning Campus
    Information Units for the Era of Digital Libraries." In *Restructuring
    Academic Libraries: Organizational Development in the Wake of Techno-
    logical Change*, edited by Charles A. Schwartz. Chicago: Association of
    College and Research Libraries.
Dukas, Neil Bernard. 2004. *A Military History of Sovereign Hawai'i*. Honolulu:
    Mutual Publishing, 2004.
Eco, Umberto. 1983. *The Name of the Rose*. Translated by William Weaver. San
    Diego: Harcourt Brace Jovanovich.
Edgar, Neal L. 1976. "The Image of Librarianship in the Media." In *A Century
    of Service: Librarianship in the United States and Canada*, edited by Sid-
    ney L. Jackson, Eleanor B. Herling, and E. J. Josey. Chicago: American
    Library Association.
Edwards, Ralph M. 2000. "A New Central Library for Phoenix." In *Building
    Libraries for the 21st Century*, edited by T. D. Webb. Jefferson, NC:
    McFarland.
French, Wendell L., and Cecil H. Bell Jr. 1999. *Organization Development:
    Behavioral Science Interventions for Organization Improvement*. Upper
    Saddle River, NJ: Prentice Hall.
Furuhashi, Lynette. 2012. Interview. University of Hawai'i at Mānoa. July 30.
Furuta, Ken. 2012. E-mail. April 11.
Gambee, Budd L., and Ruth R. Gambee. 1976. "Facilities: Reference Services
    and Technology." In *A Century of Service: Librarianship in the United
    States and Canada*, edited by Sidney L. Jackson, Eleanor B. Herling,
    and E. J. Josey. Chicago: American Library Association.
Garrison, Dee. 1979. *Apostles of Culture: The Public Librarian and American
    Society, 1876–1920*. New York: Free Press.

Gayton, Jeffrey T. 2008. "Academic Libraries: 'Social' or 'Communal?' The
	Nature and Future of Academic Libraries." *Journal of Academic
	Librarianship* 34 (1): 60–66.

Giles, Jim. 2005. "Internet Encyclopaedias Go Head to Head." *Nature* 438
	(7070): 900–901.

Gorman, Michael. 2003. *The Enduring Library: Technology, Tradition, and the
	Quest for Balance.* Chicago: American Library Association.

Green, Harriett. 2012. Interview. University of Illinois at Urbana-Champaign.
	September 12.

Grimes, Deborah J. 1998. *Academic Library Centrality: User Success through
	Service, Access, and Tradition.* Chicago: Association of College and
	Research Libraries.

Gromatzky, Steven E. 2002. "Academic Librarians 2012: Researchers, Technol-
	ogists and Proactive Partners." http://alpha.fdu.edu/~marcum
	/gromatzky.doc.

Hall, Steven. 2005. "From Paper to .PDF: Migration and Meaning in Digital
	Resources." In *Migrations in Society, Culture, and the Library: WESS
	European Conference, Paris, 2004,* edited by Tom Kilton and Ceres
	Birkhead. Chicago: Association of College and Research Libraries.

Hamlin, Arthur T. 1981. *The University Library in the United States.* Philadel-
	phia: University of Pennsylvania Press.

Haraway, Donna Jeanne. 1991. "A Cyborg Manifesto: Science, Technology,
	and Socialist-Feminism in the Late Twentieth Century." In *Simians,
	Cyborgs, and Women: The Reinvention of Nature.* New York: Routledge.

Harris, Paul. 2009. "Will California Become America's First Failed State?"
	Guardian, October 3. www.guardian.co.uk/world/2009/oct/04
	/california-failing-state-debt.

Hensley, Merinda. 2012. Interview. University of Illinois at Urbana-
	Champaign. September 12.

Hildenbrand, Suzanne. 1996. *Reclaiming the American Library Past: Writing the
	Women In.* Norwood, NJ: Ablex.

Hinchliffe, Lisa Janicke. 2007. *State of the Undergraduate Library, 2006–2007.*
	University of Illinois at Urbana-Champaign. www
	.library.illinois.edu/committee/exec/supplement/2007-2008
	/State_of_the_Undergraduate_Library.pdf.

Holmes, Leilani. 2000. "Heart Knowledge, Blood Memory, and the Voice of
	the Land: Implications of Research among Hawai'ian Elders." In
	Indigenous Knowledges in Global Contexts: Multiple Readings of

Our World, edited by George J. Sefa Dei, Budd L. Hall, and Dorothy
    Goldin Rosenberg. Toronto: University of Toronto Press.

Jackson, Sidney L. 1974. *Libraries and Librarianship in the West*. New York:
    McGraw-Hill.

Jacobs, Gwen. 2012. Interview. University of Hawai'i at Mānoa. July 16.

Jacoby, JoAnn. 2012. Interview. University of Illinois at Urbana-Champaign.
    September 12.

Johnson, L., A. Levine, R. Smith, and S. Stone. 2010. *The 2010 Horizon Report*.
    Austin, TX: New Media Consortium. www.educause.edu/library
    /resources/2010-horizon-report.

Kaser, David. 1997. *The Evolution of the American Academic Library Building*.
    Lanham, MD: Scarecrow Press.

Kaser, David, and Ruth Jackson. 1976. "Personnel." In *A Century of Service:
    Librarianship in the United States and Canada*, edited by Sidney L.
    Jackson, Eleanor B. Herling, and E. J. Josey. Chicago: American
    Library Association.

Kaufman, Paula. 2007. "It's Not Your Parents' Library Anymore." *Journal of
    Library Administration* 46 (1): 5–26.

———. 2010. "2010 State-of-the-Library." University of Illinois at Urbana-
    Champaign. www.library.illinois.edu/administration/librarian
    /State-of-the-Library/2010StateoftheLibrary.html.

———. 2012. Interview. University of Illinois at Urbana-Champaign. Septem-
    ber 10.

Kessler, Mark. 2011. "Windows into Civility: Discourse and Concourse."
    University of California, Davis. http://civilityproject.ucdavis.edu
    /Windows_Discourse_Concourse.pdf.

———. 2012. "Assignment 2—Redesign of Reference Area in Shields Library."
    University of California, Davis.

Keys, Marshall. 1999. "The Evolving Virtual Library: A Vision through a Glass,
    Darkly." In *The Evolving Virtual Library II: Practical and Philosophical
    Perspectives*, edited by Laverna M. Saunders. Medford, NJ: Informa-
    tion Today.

King, Valery, Jane Nichols, Greg Padilla, and Christopher N. Cox. 2006.
    "Moving Back to Campus: Creating a Local Virtual Reference Service."
    Internet Reference Services Quarterly 11 (3): 1–17.

Knieval, Jennifer D., Heather Wicht, and Lynn Silipigni Connaway. 2006. "Use
    of Circulation Statistics and Interlibrary Load Data in Collection
    Management." *College & Research Libraries* 67 (1).

Kolowich, Steve. 2009. "Libraries of the Future." *Inside Higher Ed*, September
    24. www.insidehighered.com/news/2009/09/24/libraries.

Kranich, Nancy. 2001. "Libraries, the Internet, and Democracy." In *Libraries and Democracy: The Cornerstones of Liberty*, edited by Nancy Kranich. Chicago: American Library Association.

Kyrillidou, Martha, and Les Bland. 2008. *ARL Statistics 2006–2007*. Washington, DC: Association of Research Libraries.

———. 2009. *ARL Statistics 2007–2008*. Washington, DC: Association of Research Libraries.

Kyrillidou, Martha, and Mark Young. 2008. *ARL Statistics 2005–2006*. Washington, DC: Association of Research Libraries.

Kyrillidou, Martha, and Shaneka Morris. 2011. *ARL Statistics 2008–2009*. Washington, DC: Association of Research Libraries.

Kyrillidou, Martha, Shaneka Morris, and Gary Roebuck. 2011. *ARL Statistics 2009–2010*. Washington, DC: Association of Research Libraries.

Lapidus, Mariana, and Irena Bond. 2009. "Virtual Reference: Chat with Us!" *Medical Reference Services Quarterly* 28 (2): 133–142.

Lee, Hyung. 2009. "Kindles Yet to Woo University Users." *Daily Princetonian*, September 28. www.dailyprincetonian.com/2009/09/28/23918/.

Levrault, Bethany R. 2006. "Integration in Academic Reference Departments: From Print to Digital Resources." *Acquisitions Librarian* 18 (35/36): 21–36.

Li, Xiaoli. 2012. Interview. University of California, Davis. June 5.

Lin, Emily. 2010. "Next-Generation Technical Services (NGTS): New Modes for Organizing and Providing Access to Special Collections, Archive, and Digital Formats." Final Report. http://libraries .universityofcalifornia.edu/about/uls/ngts/docs/NGTS2_New _Modes_FinalReport.pdf.

———. 2012. Interview. University of California, Merced. June 13.

Lin, Emily S., and R. Bruce Miller. 2004. "Japanese Fine Art: Building a Digital Enterprise while Building a New University." Presentation. Pacific Rim Digital Library Alliance. www.prdla.org/2004/10/japanese-fine -art-building-a-digital-enterprise-while-building-a-new-university/.

Lingley, Kate. 2012. Interview. University of Hawai'i at Mānoa. July 20.

Lippincott, Joan K., and Stacey Greenwell. 2011. "7 Things You Should Know about the Modern Learning Commons." *Educause*, April 11. www.educause.edu/Resources /7ThingsYouShouldKnowAbouttheMo/227141.

Loder, Michael Wescott. 2010. "Libraries with a Future: How Are Academic Library Usage and Green Demands Changing Building Designs?" *College & Research Libraries* 71 (4): 348–360.

Lollini, Thomas. 2012. Interview. University of California, Merced. June 21.

Lynch, Beverly P., and Kimberley Robles Smith. 2001. "The Changing Nature of Work in Academic Libraries." *College & Research Libraries* 62 (5): 407–420.

MacWhinnie, Laurie A. 2003. "The Information Commons: The Academic Library of the Future." *Portal: Libraries and the Academy* 3 (2): 241–257.

Madsen, Gretchen. 2012. Interview. University of Illinois at Urbana-Champaign. September 11.

Maness, Jack M. 2006. "Library 2.0 Theory: Web 2.0 and Its Implications for Libraries." *Webology* 3 (2). www.webology.org/2006/v3n2/a25.html.

Massie, Robert K. 1980. *Peter the Great: His Life and World*. New York: Knopf.

McGuigan, Glenn S. 2004. "Publishing Perils in Academe: The Serials Crisis and the Economics of the Academic Journal Publishing Industry." *Journal of Business & Finance Librarianship* 10 (1): 13–26.

McPherson, James M. 1988. *Battle Cry of Freedom: The Civil War Era*. New York: Oxford University Press.

Meder, Steve. 2012. Interview. University of Hawai'i at Mānoa. July 24.

Meister, Marcia. 2012. Interview. University of California, Davis. May 8.

Mestre, Lori. 2012. Interview. University of Illinois at Urbana-Champaign. September 10.

Michalski, David. 2011a. "New Trends in Reference Service." University of California, Davis.

———. 2011b. "We Are the Crisis: Students as Consumers, Market Mediation, and the Coming Role of Reference." Paper presented at Fiat Flux: Changing Universities, Challenges for Libraries, Berkeley, California, October 21.

———. 2012. Interview. University of California, Davis. May 4.

Mikkelsen, Susan. 2012. Interview. University of California, Merced. June 11.

Mochida, Paula. 2012. Interview. University of Hawai'i at Mānoa. July 19.

Naya, Seiji F. 2000. "Preface." In *Hawai'i's Emerging New Economy: A Progress Report*. Honolulu, HI.

Neary, Lynn. 2011. "The Future of Libraries in the E-Book Age." NPR, April 4. www.npr.org/2011/04/04/135117829 /the-future-of-libraries-in-the-e-book-age.

Newman, David. 2010. "The Adaptive Organization: How Boyd's Decision Cycle and Pattern-Based Strategy Drive Rapid Change." Gartner Research, October 5.

Norman, Michael. 2012. Interview. University of Illinois at Urbana-Champaign. September 11.

O'Brien, Nancy. 2012. Interview. University of Illinois at Urbana-Champaign. September 11.

O'Gorman, Jack, and Barry Trott. 2009. "What Will Become of Reference in Academic and Public Libraries?" *Journal of Library Administration* 49 (4): 327–339.

O'Neill, Edward T., and Julia A. Gammon. 2009. "Building Collections Cooperatively: Analysis of Collection Use in the OhioLINK Library Consortium." Paper presented at ACRL 2009—Pushing the Edge: Explore, Engage, Extend (14th national conference), Seattle, WA, March 12–15.

Oakleaf, Megan. 2010. *Value of Academic Libraries: A Comprehensive Research Review and Report.* Chicago: Association of College and Research Libraries.

Overall, Patricia Montiel. 2009. "Cultural Competence: A Conceptual Framework for Library and Information Science Professionals." *Library Quarterly* 79 (2): 175–204.

Pinfield, Stephen, Jonathan Eaton, Catherine Edwards, Rosemary Russell, Astrid Wissenburg, and Peter Wynne. 1998. "Realizing the Hybrid Library." *D-Lib Magazine.* www.dlib.org/dlib/october98/10pinfield.html.

Polansky, Patricia. 2012. Interview. University of Hawaiʻi at Mānoa. July 26.

Posner, Beth. n.d. "Is There a Librarian in the House?" www.docstoc.com/docs/68034493/posner.

R2 Consulting LCC. 2009. "University of Hawaiʻi at Mānoa Library: Workflow and Organizational Analysis, June 2009." Draft Report. http://library.manoa.hawaii.edu/about/R2HIWorkflowRpt2009.pdf.

Rader, Hannelore B. 1999. "Information Literacy in the Reference Environment: Preparing for the Future." *Reference Librarian* 31 (66): 213.

Ralph, Lynette L., and Timothy J. Ellis. 2009. "An Investigation of a Knowledge Management Solution for the Improvement of Reference Services." *Journal of Information, Information Technology, and Organizations* 4: 17–38.

Rettig, James. 2002. "Technology, Cluelessness, Anthropology, and the Memex: The Future of Academic Reference Service." *Reference Services Review* (1): 17–21.

Rider, Fremont. 1944. *The Scholar and the Future of the Research Library.* New York: Hadham Press.

Rogers, A. Robert. 1976. "Library Buildings." In *A Century of Service: Librarianship in the United States and Canada,* edited by Sidney L. Jackson, Eleanor B. Herling, and E. J. Josey. Chicago: American Library Association.

Rothstein, Samuel. 1976. "Service in Academia." In *A Century of Service: Librarianship in the United States and Canada*, edited by Sidney L. Jackson, Eleanor B. Herling, and E. J. Josey. Chicago: American Library Association.

Roy, Loriene. 2009. "Indigenous Matters in Library and Information Sccience: An Evolving Ecology." *Focus in International Library and Information Work* 40 (2): 8–12.

Roy, Loriene, and Antony Cherian. 2004. "Indigenous Peoples and Information Technology." In *From Outreach to Equity: Innovative Models of Library Policy and Practice*, edited by Robin Osborne. Chicago: American Library Association.

Roy, Loriene, and Kristen Hogan. 2010. "We Collect, Organize, Preserve, and Provide Access, with Respect: Indigenous Peoples' Cultural Life in Libraries." In *Beyond Article 19: Libraries and Social and Cultural Rights*, edited by Julie Biando Edwards and Stephan P. Edwards. Duluth, MN: Library Juice Press.

Rudin, Phyllis. 2008. "No Fixed Address: The Evolution of Outreach Library Services on University Campuses." *Reference Librarian* 49 (1): 55–75.

Rutter, Sara. 2012. Interview. University of Hawai'i at Mānoa. July 16.

Sandore, Beth. 2012. Interview. University of Illinois at Urbana-Champaign. September 12.

Saunders, Laverna M. 1999. "The Virtual Library: Reflections on an Evolutionary Process." In *The Evolving Virtual Library II*, edited by Laverna M. Saunders. Medford, NJ: Information Today.

Schabas, Ann H. 1976. "Technical Services and Technology: Technological Advance." In *A Century of Service: Librarianship in the United States and Canada*, edited by Sidney L. Jackson, Eleanor B. Herling, and E. J. Josey. Chicago: American Library Association.

Scherrei, Rita A. 1997. "Caught in the Crossfire: Organizational Change and Career Displacement in the University of California Libraries." In *Restructuring Academic Libraries: Organizational Development in the Wake of Technological Change*, edited by Charles A. Schwartz. Chicago: Association of College and Research Libraries.

Scheuring, Ann F. 2001. *Abundant Harvest: The History of the University of California, Davis*. Davis: UC Davis History Project.

Schottlaender, Brian E. C. 2009. "Future Staff: Thoughts on Identity with Deductive Corroboration." Presentation at the University of California, Irvine.

Scott, Eric. 2012. Interview. University of California at Merced. June 11.

Seaman, David. 2005. "The Migrated Library: Distributed, Malleable, En-
    meshed, Immediate." In *Migrations in Society, Culture, and the Library:
    WESS European Conference, Paris, 2004*, edited by Tom Kilton
    and Ceres Birkhead. Chicago: Association of College and Research
    Libraries.

Searing, Susan E. 2009. "The 'Librarian's Library' in Transition from Physical
    to Virtual Place: A Case Study of the Library & Information Science
    Library at the University of Illinois, USA." Paper presented at IFLA
    satellite conference, Libraries as Space and Place, Torino, Italy, August
    20.

———. 2012. Interview. University of Illinois at Urbana-Champaign. Septem-
    ber 20.

Searing, Susan E., and Alison M. Greenlee. 2011. "Faculty Responses to
    Library Service Innovations: A Case Study." *Journal of Education for
    Library and Information Science* 52 (4): 279–294.

Seiden, Peggy. 1997. "Restructuring Liberal Arts College Libraries: Seven
    Organizational Strategies." In *Restructuring Academic Libraries: Orga-
    nizational Development in the Wake of Technological Change*, edited by
    Charles A. Schwartz. Chicago: Association of College and Research
    Libraries.

Sheedy, J. E. 2007. "The Physiology of Eyestrain." *Journal of Modern Optics* 54
    (9): 1333–1341.

Shepley Bulfinch Richardson & Abbott. 2006. "University of Illinois at Urbana-
    Champaign: Conceptual Framework Report." Executive Summary.
    www.library.illinois.edu/administration/services
    /planning/renovation/SBRA_Conceptual_Framework_2006.pdf.

Shill, Harold B., and Shawn Tonner. 2003. "Creating a Better Place: Physical
    Improvements in Academic Libraries, 1995–2002." *College & Research
    Libraries* 64 (6): 431–466.

———. 2004. "Does the Building Still Matter? Usage Patterns in New,
    Expanded, and Renovated Libraries, 1995–2002." *College & Research
    Libraries* 65 (2): 123–150.

Shreeves, Sarah. 2012. Interview. University of Illinois at Urbana-Champaign.
    September 11.

Siegel, Adam. 2012. Interview. University of California, Davis. March 15.

Sinclair, Gwen. 2012. Interview. University of Hawai'i at Mānoa. July 20.

Smith, Linda. 2012. Interview. University of Illinois at Urbana-Champaign.
    September 11.

Smith, MacKenzie. 2013. Interview. University of California, Davis. January 22.

Smith, Teal. 2012. Interview. University of California, Merced. June 11.

Solberg, Winton U. 2000. *The University of Illinois 1894–1904: The Shaping of the University*. Urbana: University of Illinois Press.

———. 2004. "Edmund Janes James Builds a Library: The University of Illinois Library, 1904–1920." *Libraries & Culture* 39 (1): 36–75.

Stoffle, Carla, Barbara Allen, David Morden, and Krisellen Maloney. 2003. "Continuing to Build the Future: Academic Libraries and Their Challenges." *Portal: Libraries and the Academy* 3 (3): 360–380.

Strasser, Carly. 2012. Interview. University of California, Davis. October 31.

Systemwide Operations and Planning Advisory Group (SOPAG). 2011. "SOPAG: NGTS Implementation Initiative Framework." University of California Libraries, April 21. http://libraries .universityofcalifornia.edu/ngts/documents.

Thompson, James. 1977. *A History of the Principles of Librarianship*. London: Clive Bingley.

Titangos, Hui-Lan, and Deborah Jan. 2007. "Library Innovations in the 21st Century: An International Perspective." *Chinese Librarianship: An International Electronic Journal* 1 (23).

Tocqueville, Alexis de. 1840. *Democracy in America*. Vol. 2. Citation is to the translation by George Lawrence. New York: HarperPerennial, 1969.

Tomlinson-Keasey, Carol. 2007. "A Delicate Dance." *New Directions for Higher Education*, no. 139 (Fall): 13–26.

Tooey, Mary Joan. 2010. "Renovated, Repurposed, and Still 'One Sweet Library': A Case Study on Loss of Space from the Health Sciences and Human Services Library." *Journal of the Medical Library Association* 98 (1): 40–43.

Trilling, Renée. 2012. Interview. University of Illinois at Urbana-Champaign. September 19.

UC Merced Library. 2011. "Annual Assessment Plan 2011–2012." http:// ucmercedlibrary.info/images/stories/pdf/UC-Merced -Library-Annual-Assessment-Plan-Final.pdf.

Underwood, Ted. 2012. Interview. University of Illinois at Urbana-Champaign. September 20.

Underwood, Ted, and Jordan Sellers. 2012. "The Emergence of Literary Diction." *Journal of Digital Humanities* 1 (2).

University of California, Davis. 2012. "Meet the New University Librarian." Accessed January 23. www.lib.ucdavis.edu/ul/about/meetnewul.php.

University of California, Merced. 2009. "UC Merced Tomorrow: Long Range Development Plan." Final Report. http://lrdp.ucmerced .edu/2.asp?uc=1&lvl2=49&contentid=50.

University of California Libraries. 1992–2012. UC Library Annual Statistics.
    http://libraries.universityofcalifornia.edu/about/facts-and-figures.
University of Hawaiʻi at Mānoa. 2007. "Long Range Development Plan:
    University of Hawaiʻi, Mānoa Campus." 2007 Update. Group 70
    International. http://manoa.hawaii.edu/planning/LRDP/lrdp.html.
———. 2008. "Campus Guide: University of Hawaiʻi at Mānoa." Office of
    Admissions.
———. 2011. "Achieving Our Destiny: The University of Hawaiʻi at Mānoa,
    2011–2015 Strategic Plan." http://manoa.hawaii.edu/vision/.
University of Hawaiʻi at Mānoa Library. 2012. "Open Access Policy." Office of
    the Vice Chancellor for Academic Affairs. http://library.manoa
    .hawaii.edu/about/scholcom/oa-policy.htm.
Valeho-Novikoff, Shanye. 2012. Interview. University of Hawaiʻi at Mānoa.
    July 19.
Ward, David. 2012. Interview. University of Illinois at Urbana-Champaign.
    September 11.
Webb, T. D. 2000a. "Conclusion." In *Building Libraries for the 21st Century:
    The Shape of Information*, edited by T. D. Webb. Jefferson, NC:
    McFarland.
———. 2000b. "Introduction." In *Building Libraries for the 21st Century*.
Weech, Terry. 2012. Interview. University of Illinois at Urbana-Champaign.
    September 10.
Weiler, Angela. 2005. "Information-Seeking Behavior in Generation Y Stu-
    dents: Motivation, Critical Thinking, and Learning Theory." *Journal of
    Academic Librarianship* 31 (1): 46–53.
Weppler-Selear, Mary. 2012. Interview. University of California, Merced.
    September 13.
Wertheimer, Andrew. 2012. Interview. University of Hawaiʻi, Mānoa. July 23.
Wheeler, Richard. 2012. Interview. University of Illinois at Urbana-
    Champaign. September 12.
White, Marilyn Domas. 2001. "Diffusion of an Innovation: Digital Reference
    Service in Carnegie Foundation Master's (Comprehensive) Academic
    Institution Libraries." *Journal of Academic Librarianship* 27 (3):
    173–187.
Wiegand, Wayne A. 1996. *A Biography of Melvil Dewey: Irrepressible Reformer*.
    Chicago: American Library Association.
Wilkin, John. 2012. E-mail. December 7.
Winston, Bonnie V., and Tom Schoenberg. 2012. "Ex-UVA Student Huguely
    Found Guilty of Murdering Girlfriend Yeardley Love." *Bloomberg*,
    February 22.

Yano, Candace Arai, Z.-J. Max Shen, and Stephen Chan. 2008. "Optimizing
    the Number of Copies for Print Preservation of Research Journals."
    Berkeley: University of California, Berkeley.
Zabel, Diane. 2007. "A Reference Renaissance." *Reference & User Services
    Quarterly* 47: 108–110.

Image Credits

■■

Page 7: Photograph courtesy of the University of Illinois, American Library Association Archives.

Page 64: From official ARL Statistics (Kyrillidou and Bland 2008, 2009; Kyrillidou and Morris 2011; Kyrillidou, Morris, and Roebuck 2011; Kyrillidou and Young 2008).

Page 66, *top*: Courtesy of Ken Furuta.

Page 66, *bottom*: Courtesy of Ken Furuta.

Page 70: Reproduced with permission from The Regents of the University of California, Davis campus, © 2009. All rights reserved.

Page 71: Reproduced with permission from The Regents of the University of California, Davis campus, © 2009. All rights reserved.

Page 72: MD Consult (First Consult and MD Consult are medical research tools owned by the publisher Elsevier).

Page 74: Reproduced with permission from the Trustees of Dartmouth College and Yale University, © 2006. All rights reserved. Produced by Jan Glover, David Izzo, Karen Odato, and Lei Wang.

Page 79: Copyright of the UC Regents and available under a Creative Commons Attribution 3.0 unported license.

Page 91: © David Wakely Photography.

Page 92: Courtesy of University of California Libraries 1992–2012.

Page 106: From official ARL Statistics (Kyrillidou and Bland 2008, 2009; Kyrillidou and Morris 2011; Kyrillidou, Morris, and Roebuck 2011; Kyrillidou and Young 2008).

Page 123: Photograph by Kalev Leetaru.

Page 125: From official ARL Statistics (Kyrillidou and Bland 2008, 2009; Kyrillidou and Morris 2011; Kyrillidou, Morris, and Roebuck 2011; Kyrillidou and Young 2008).

Page 131: Photograph by Don Hamerman.

Index

⊞

Locators in italic refer to figures and tables. The following abbreviations are used below: